# Lessons from the
# Great Depression

# Lessons from the Great Depression

## The Lionel Robbins Lectures for 1989

Peter Temin

The MIT Press
Cambridge, Massachusetts
London, England

This book was set in 10/13pt Palatino
by Asco Trade Typesetting Ltd., Hong Kong
and printed and bound
in the United States of America.

Library of Congress Cataloging-in-Publication Data

Temin, Peter.
    Lessons from the Great Depression/Peter Temin.
        p.   cm.—(Lionel Robbins lectures)
    Bibliography: p.
    Includes index.
    ISBN 0-262-20073-2
    1. Depressions—1929—Great Britain.   2. Depressions—1929—
France.   3. Depressions—1929—Germany.   4. Depressions—1929—
United States.   I. Title.   II. Series.
    HB3717   1929.T45      1989
    330.9'0437—dc20                                    89-34040
                                                          CIP

For Charlotte

# Contents

# Foreword

Europe today is in the biggest recession since the 1930s, with unemployment over 10 percent. The position of the debt-ridden countries of the Third World is still worse. In consequence the world economy has grown more slowly in the 1980s than in the rest of the postwar period.

This raises the questions, Why? And what can be done about it? A natural way to throw light on these issues is to look back at the Great Depression of the 1930s. What caused it, and what brought it to an end?

So we were delighted when Peter Temin of MIT agreed to give the fourth annual series of Lionel Robbins Memorial Lectures, and to give them on this subject. He is not only one of the world's leading economic historians but an expert on this particular issue. In this book he builds on his previous book *Did Monetary Forces Cause the Great Depression?* and synthesizes the large economic literature that has been written on the Great Depression since then.

Temin offers an integrated view of the cause, spread, and recovery from the Great Depression. He uses a sequence of consistent economic models to explain events within a unified Keynesian model of the international economy. The account shows both how economic models can be applied to the past and how the lessons of the past can be applied to the present.

Temin argues in the first chapter that the Depression was the result of an unyielding commitment to the gold standard in circumstances for which it was no longer appropriate. The event that outmoded the gold standard was the First World War, which initiated international conflict lasting beyond the war itself. But the costs of returning to the prewar financial arrangements only emerged in the late 1920s. The deflationary bias of gold-standard ideology was exactly the wrong medicine for the world economy at this time.

Economic policies, not structural problems of the interwar economy, produced the Depression. It was not the accident of one man's death or the absence of international cooperation but rather the commitment to an archaic policy. Modern parallels are found in the deflationary policies of the United States and Britain after 1979, which were relaxed in time to avoid a financial collapse, and in the continued adherence of the current American administration to inappropriate policies.

In the second chapter Temin argues that the Depression was so deep because of the unyielding commitment to the gold standard on the part of fiscal and monetary authorities in the large industrial countries. They held to contractionary policies in an attempt to deflate their economies and restore international equilibrium. They succeeded only in the first of these aims. The downturn became the Great Depression as a result of the continuation of deflationary policies long after the economic decline was undery way.

This chapter extends the logic of the first chapter, showing how the inability to adapt economic policies to new conditions can lead to disaster. Expectations played a crucial role, first by not anticipating the depth of the Depression and then by anticipating further deflation and troubles. Expectations were not "rational" in the modern sense because the Depression was a new phenomenon and the economic models to explain it were in their infancy. We need to be wary of policies made today that assume that policymakers and investors understand more than they actually do. Temin argues in the third chapter that recovery was initiated by the introduction of new, expansive macroeconomic policy regimes in the United States and Germany. He argues that these regimes, joined later by France and still later by Britain, were socialist in nature, combining management of the economy with concern for workers. Although perverted by the Nazis, the socialist impulse gathered strength after the Second World War, leading to an era of democratic socialism which is now coming to an end.

These new regimes were introduced only after the economic decline had continued for several years. The historical narrative does not hold out much hope for speedy adoption of new regimes. It reveals the parallel between the continuation of high unemployment in Europe today and the American unemployment under Roosevelt. Temin speculates tha the cost of high unemployment may be offset by more rapid technical progress in these conditions.

This is thus a highly topical book. It is an expert interpretation of how the capitalist system can go wrong if people fail to understand its workings. The Lionel Robbins Memorial Trust is extremely grateful to Peter Temin for this stimulating contribution. The debate began when Lionel Robbins was himself a young man and the events described in this book were taking place. And it will continue. But Peter Temin has crystallized the issues and their relevance to today in a way that no one else could have done.

Richard Layard

work was not written in the heat of the moment. I continue to think that my previous work is fundamentally sound. Sound, but slightly antiquated. The answers are fine; it is the questions that are dated. In particular, my book was written at the height of the debate over whether monetary or fiscal policy is ineffective. The fire has gone out of that controversy; anyone who has lived through Paul Volcker's deflationary monetary policy and then Ronald Reagan's expansionary fiscal policy must agree that both policies have effects on the economy (Boskin 1988). The questions I want to pose here are more general questions about the origins, spread, and end of the Great Depression. These questions involve policy regimes and expectations, and they emphasize the international aspect of the Depression. Friedman and Schwartz set the stage for my earlier research, Kindleberger and Eichengreen (working independently) have provided the context for these lectures.

My aim in these lectures is to provide an integrated view of the Great Depression. This requires a similarity of approach to different phases of the Depression as well as to the experiences in different countries. I will restrict my attention to Britain, France, Germany, and the United States, on the grounds that other countries were affected by events in these four countries far more than they affected them. The three lectures will treat in turn the cause of the Depression—the impulse in modern terminology—its spread, and the recovery. The body of the lectures do not require economics training to understand; appendixes detail the underlying models and regressions.

My aim in giving these lectures is twofold. As always, history is an intriguing subject. In addition, however, there is much to be learned for our time from a discussion of the Great Depression. I will draw lessons from the Great Depression for today in each of the lectures, although Clio

# Preface

I am happy to have been asked to give the Robbins Lectures for 1989. I am also pleased to discuss a subject that was of abiding interest to Robbins himself. There is even a closer parallel of some interest. Robbins wrote about the Great Depression at two times in his life. I am following this pattern, having done my previous work more than fifteen years ago.

But there the parallel ends. Robbins wrote in his second pass, in his *Autobiography*, that he regarded his views in his first pass, in the course of the Depression, "as the greatest mistake of [his] professional career." He wrote that he regarded his book, *The Great Depression*, "as something which I would willingly see forgotten." He continued, "Re-reading it recently—it involved a considerable effort to screw myself up to this—I found much incidental matter which seems to me well put and well argued . . . but whatever there is of good is vitiated by [a] fundamental misconception" (Robbins 1971, pp. 154–155).

I will describe Robbins' fundamental misconception in the course of the lectures, where I will argue that he was not alone in his views. Now I want simply to say that I do not regard my earlier work in the same light that Robbins saw his. It has not been as long an interval, and my earlier (the muse of history) is like the Delphic Oracle. She is both articulate and ambiguous.

I want to thank several people for help in writing these lectures. Betty Krier provided able research assistance. Theodore Balderston, Knut Borchardt, Bradford De Long, Barry Eichengreen, Thomas Ferguson, Timothy Hatton, Harold James, Charles Kindleberger, Bradford Lee, Stephen Schuker, Eugene White, and Robert Zevin all were kind enough to give me extremely thoughtful comments. They illustrated once again the joys of participating in the community of scholars. I alone must take responsibility for resisting their efforts to keep me on the straight and narrow.

.

# Lessons from the Great Depression

# 1      The Spoils of War: The Cause of the Great Depression

The Depression of the 1930s was a watershed in the history of modern economies. But it was one aspect of a major watershed in world history, what Churchill termed the "Second Thirty Years' War" (Churchill 1948, p. xiii). Lionel Robbins foreshadowed this view at the time he wrote his book on the Depression in 1933. Even though he obviously could not see the end of this convulsion, he did recognize its start. He therefore began his analysis by proclaiming, "We live, not in the fourth, but in the nineteenth year of the world crisis" (Robbins 1934, p. 1).

This view is instructive and one that I want to keep in mind, because it places the Depression in historical context. The origins of the Great Depression lie largely in the disruptions of the First World War. Its spread owes much to the hostilities and continuing conflicts that were created by the war and the Treaty of Versailles. And its effects—particularly the victory of National Socialism in Germany—clearly extend to the Second World War. It is instructive to see the thirty years following 1914 as one long conflict with an uneasy truce in the middle.

This makes the Great Depression unusual in its historical context, but it does not thereby make it irrelevant to current events. Indeed, the interaction of economics and poli-

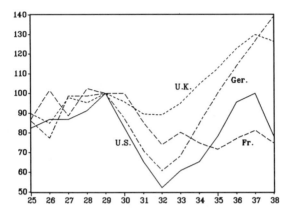

**Figure 1.1**
Industrial production in four countries (1929 = 100). Sources:
Mitchell (1980, pp. 376–377); Federal Reserve System (1940).

tics that is central to my story of the Depression is a constant of economic and political life. And it is within the realm of possibility that politicians would again make choices that would lead into another Great Depression. I will suggest later how a leader who is determined to produce a depression might act.

Economists often eschew the broad brush of the historian. Although I will attempt to avoid that failing, I want to employ a more restricted point of view as well. I will attempt to strike a balance between the large themes of the historian and the intricate analysis of the economist. Turning to the latter view, the Depression can be seen as a fluctuation in the level of aggregate production in the principal industrial economies. Even this restrained view shows the Depression to be extraordinary. Figure 1.1 shows the path of industrial production for Britain, France, Germany, and the United States from 1925 to 1938. (The dates are dictated by the limits of the German data; the indexes are normalized around 1929.)

**Table 1.1**
Industrial unemployment rates

| Country | 1921–29 | 1930–38 | Average Rate | Difference | Ratio of difference to average |
|---|---|---|---|---|---|
| United States | 7.9 | 26.1 | 17 | 18.2 | 1.07 |
| United Kingdom | 12 | 15.4 | 13.7 | 3.4 | 0.25 |
| France | 3.8 | 10.2 | 7 | 6.4 | 0.91 |
| Germany | 9.2 | 21.8 | 15.5 | 12.6 | 0.81 |

Source: Eichengreen and Hatton (1988).

It is still disputed whether the economy was more stable after the Second Thirty Years' War than before the First, but no one disputes the extent of volatility in the "interwar" truce (Romer 1986). The graph shows that the United States, France, and Germany were more volatile than the United Kingdom. This does not imply, of course, that foregone output in this period was smaller for Britain than for these other countries. Britain only spread its unemployment over a longer span.

Table 1.1 contains estimates of industrial unemployment rates for the 1920s and 1930s (Eichengreen and Hatton 1988). France, not Britain, was the outlier by this index, having the lowest average industrial unemployment for the interwar years. The low French unemployment rates may be a statistical artifact; more likely, they show the prevalence of underemployment in a still traditional and agricultural France. The high German rates reflect in part the volatility of insured employment in that country.

Britain was the outlier in a comparison of the two decades. The last column shows the difference between the industrial unemployment rates in the 1930s and 1920s as a ratio to the average rate for both decades. The ratio is about one for three countries; unemployment rates roughly doubled between the 1920s and the 1930s. The ratio for Britain

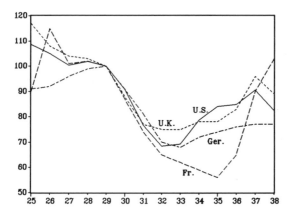

**Figure 1.2**
Wholesale prices in four countries (1929 = 100). Sources: Mitchell
(1980, pp. 774–775); U.S. Bureau of the Census (1975, p. 200).

is completely different; industrial unemployment in the
1930s was only one-quarter larger than in the 1920s.

These data clearly do not suggest the presence of strong
forces pushing national economies toward full employment. A time-series analysis of the monthly data for the
United States shows that industrial production in this
country followed a random walk (Federal Reserve System
1940). Without trying to characterize formally the underlying process that generated this result, let me say only
that it shows the persistent effects of the major macroeconomic shocks in those years. These lectures will try to explain in turn what the shocks were, how they spread, and
why their effects endured so long.

Figure 1.2 shows the price level in the same four countries. Price movements in these four countries were even
more similar than the changes in production. In fact there
was a surprisingly common rate of deflation among these
countries from 1929 to 1931. This massive international deflationary movement—a 20 percent fall in two years—is a
key part of the story of the Great Depression.

The intellectual framework for this story combines history and economics. The historical paradigm is international and concerned with the interaction of economics and politics. Even technical decisions by expert monetary and fiscal authorities, I shall argue, are part of a unified historical process determining individual and national destinies.

The economic framework draws on modern macroeconomic theory at three levels. First, I plan to analyze the Depression within the impulse-propagation framework of modern macroeconomics. This distinction originates in the construction of time-series models. Structural equations typically are a combination of deterministic relations among variables and a stochastic error (that may be a function of other variables as well). Movements in the error term are considered to be impulses, innovations, or shocks. They are the exogenous changes that move the system. The dynamic properties of the deterministic system then determine how the system responds to a given shock, that is, how an impulse is propagated throughout the model economy.

Second, modern macroeconomics distinguishes between actions and regimes. The latter are the underlying principles of policy that determine most actions. The randomness in policy actions makes it hard to infer the regime from observation of actions. But if we ignore that problem, investors and traders will not need to react to individual actions undertaken within a given regime. They will have anticipated most of them in their actions already. The unanticipated actions will be interpreted as noise, and the economic decision makers will not respond to noise (Lucas 1981; Sargent 1986).

Third, explicit models will be introduced as the discussion progresses, although the analysis may draw on more than one model at a time. I argue in appendix A, where the individual models are set out formally, that these models are all consistent extensions of a basic IS-LM framework. They can be combined for the analysis of this complex historical event, even though the formal expression of a grand unified model would be unwieldy (see Solow 1985, for a description of this methodology).

The framework for the discussion in this lecture is a standard aggregate supply/aggregate demand model in which the IS curve responds to relative international prices and to the interest rate. Introduced by Eichengreen and Sachs (1985, 1986) to analyze the role of devaluations in the recovery of the 1930s, it can be extended to deal with the expansion of the 1920s as well (Eichengreen 1986b).

Adoption of the impulse-propagation structure has an immediate implication. The Depression was a major macroeconomic event. It consequently must have been the result of either a major shock or a magnifying—unstable—propagation process; a small impulse to a stable system does not produce a major depression. Most of the literature of the past decade has chosen the latter alternative. Research on the propagation mechanism has attempted to show that the economy was indeed far less stable in 1930 than before the First World War.

I want to argue a contrary view: that the impulse for the Depression was very powerful, that the Great Depression was the result of a large shock. There is no evidence that the world economy was peculiarly unstable between the wars. It is only because no large shocks have been identified that this view has emerged. I want to reverse the balance in the recent literature between impulse and propagation. I will, in other words, argue that the interwar economy was subject to major deflationary shocks. This will necessitate more discussion of politics and history than is usual in economic discourse. It will also require consideration of interwar events as part of the conflicts that made up the Second Thirty Years' War.

Keynes was quite clear in his mind about the impulse that set off the Depression. He said in mid-1931 that in "the fall of investment. . . I find—and I find without any doubt or reserves whatsoever—the whole of the explanation of the present state of affairs." The fall in investment was due in turn to a complex of causes: high interest rates, diminishing returns to investment, tight Federal Reserve policies, gold scarcity outside the United States, and falling American foreign investment. Keynes listed the last two items as the results of the Federal Reserve's tightness; the first (high interest rates) similarly was a reflection of contractionary policies in the United States and other countries. With the exception of one rather elusive item, diminishing returns to investment, Keynes' complex of causes therefore collapses into one: restrictionary monetary policy (Keynes 1931, pp. 349–351).

Rephrasing this conclusion, Keynes argued that the deflationary impulse was monetary policy and that this impulse propagated through its impact on investment. His interest—like his modern-day followers and critics—was in the propagating mechanism, and he consequently did not examine more closely his candidate for the shock. He returned over and over again in the years leading up to *The General Theory* to the effects of changes in investment, that is, to the propagation of deflationary impulses, but he virtually ignored the historical impulse itself.

I follow Keynes here and assign a primary role to tight monetary policy in the late 1920s. But I want to take the argument one step further. The tight monetary—and fiscal—policies of the late 1920s were due to the adherence of policymakers to the ideology of the gold standard. Choices made by monetary and fiscal authorities in the

years around 1930 were made according to a view of the
world that said that maintenance of the gold standard—
such as it was by the late 1920s—was the primary pre-
requisite for prosperity. As a result of this ideology, monetary and fiscal authorities implemented contractionary
policies when the clarity of hindsight shows us clearly
that expansionary policies were needed.

The ideology that determined specific actions was a policy *regime*. It indicated a stable reaction to external events.
This regime was well known to observers. Both policymakers and people affected by their actions operated within
this regime. When they thought of alternative actions, they
thought of alternatives within this regime, that is, within
the gold standard. Alternatives outside this regime were
not taken seriously, whether by policymakers when proposed or by investors and consumers when undertaken.
They were interpreted as aberrations from the stable gold-
standard regime.

What was the gold standard? There does not appear to
be a single answer in the literature, despite the volume of
work on the operation and effect of this system. Following
Dam (1982, ch. 2), I define the gold standard in terms of
five characteristics, two of which are implied by the other
three. The gold standard was characterized by (1) the free
flow of gold between individuals and countries, (2) the
maintenance of fixed values of national currencies in terms
of gold and therefore each other, and (3) the absence of an
international coordinating organization. Together, these
arrangements implied that (4) there was an asymmetry between countries experiencing balance-of-payments deficits
and surpluses. There was a penalty for running out of gold
or foreign reserves (the inability to maintain the fixed value
of the currency), but no penalty—aside from foregone interest and, possibly, inflation—for accumulating gold. In
addition (5) the adjustment mechanism for a deficit coun-

try was deflation rather than devaluation, that is, a change in domestic prices instead of a change in the exchange rate.

This last point—the choice of deflation over devaluation—can be seen clearly in Robbins' views at the depth of the Depression. He made the general statement that "a greater flexibility of wage rates would considerably reduce unemployment." He then applied this view to the Depression: "If it had not been for the prevalence of the view that wage rates must at all costs be maintained in order to maintain the purchasing power of the consumer, the violence of the present depression and the magnitude of the unemployment which has accompanied it would have been considerably less." Robbins had the wit to acknowledge that this was a "hard saying" and to insist that all prices, not just wages, needed to be flexible. These caveats do not moderate his prescription; they simply expose the depth of his conviction that internal deflation was the only way to cope with a fall in demand (Robbins 1934, p. 186). This was his "fundamental misconception."

The alternatives to the gold standard include far more than simply floating exchange rates. The Bretton Woods system, for example, did not require the free flow of gold. It employed pegged rather than fixed exchange rates, recognizing from the start that exchange values might need to be adjusted periodically to take account of changing economic conditions. And the Bretton Woods system included arrangements for an international coordinating body: the International Monetary Fund. Keynes even proposed that the responsibility for adjustment be made symmetric by charging countries for credit balances. Although not adopted due to American opposition, the proposal shows that the asymmetry of the gold standard need not be an attribute of a fixed exchange rate regime (Dam 1982, pp. 79–80, 88–92).

The gold standard, in other words, was a very particular way of organizing international financial markets. The gold exchange system of the interwar period shared with the gold system the five characteristics listed above. I therefore consider the interwar gold standard to be the gold standard, as opposed to another institutional arrangement. In particular, it smiled on the accumulation of gold balances and offered only the bitter pill of deflation to countries experiencing a drain. This prescription unhappily had side effects that made it unsafe for use in the late 1920s.

The distinction between impulse and propagation seems to be getting blurred already, for this argument makes monetary and fiscal policy part of the propagation mechanism, not the impulse as Keynes had it. In fact the gold standard regime also emerges as part of the propagating structure. It explains how economies responded to adverse shocks. But what was the shock that set the system in motion?

The shock, I want to argue, was the First World War. More broadly, the shock was the continuing conflict that made up the Second Thirty Years' War. It is a commonplace today that the gold standard was "easily destroyed in a few days in August 1914" (Dam 1982, p. 40). This view is only superficially correct. The gold standard was suspended by the major European powers during the war, but the idea of the gold standard was not so easily vanquished. The regime was unchanged. No policymaker in 1914 saw the events of that August as the end of an era. Everyone saw it instead as a temporary interruption in a stable, ongoing international framework. Brown was more insightful when he asserted in his classic study that "it is impossible to say that the gold standard was abandoned during the war" (Brown 1940, p. 165).[1]

The interruption unhappily was prolonged. Yet a cardinal aim of economic policy after the war was the reestablishment of the gold standard. Worried about a gold scarcity, the 1922 Genoa Conference acknowledged the prewar evolution of the gold standard toward a more complex arrangement where countries held reserves in both gold and foreign exchange. While the term they used, gold exchange system, was new, the practice of holding foreign-exchange reserves was not (Lindert 1969, pp. 14–15). Central bankers of the 1920s were fully aware of this.

The change was in the world economy, not the international policy regime. Britain and Germany were economically much weaker than before the war, and the United States much stronger. The course of demography, agricultural production, and international capital movements had been changed by the war. At the same exchange rate the United States and Britain had reversed foreign roles. Germany had gone from capital exporter to importer. Agriculture had gone from prosperity to poverty.

It consequently required great effort to revive the gold standard, and it took many years. But the aim of policy was clear. And when the strains of implementing this aim emerged at the end of the 1920s, monetary and fiscal authorities only redoubled their efforts. The result, as we know, was disaster.

When the shock came in 1914, the Depression did not take place because policy responses at that time were dominated by the needs of war. After the war—during the long truce between the two active conflicts—the attempt to re-establish this aspect of the *status quo ante* first created the tensions that led to contraction and then the policies that sustained the downturn.

I will describe the policies in the remainder of this lecture and argue that the gold standard was alive, although hardly well, in the minds of economic policymakers into the early 1930s. The next lecture will turn from the deflationary impulse to its propagation. (The final lecture will discuss the recovery.) It will become apparent that the economic policymakers of the 1920s and early 1930s were like the eighteenth-century doctors who treated Mozart with mercury. Not only were they singularly ineffective in curing the economic disease; they also killed the patient.

Wartime policies approximated the gold standard to the extent possible. In Britain, center of the prewar gold standard, the dollar–sterling exchange rate was pegged a year after the suspension of gold sales at $4.76, only about 2 percent below the previous par (Moggridge 1972, p. 16). Gold flowed into the United States as European hostilities spread. There was no strain on the American commitment to the gold standard, and it was not until September 1917, after the United States had entered the war, that President Wilson prohibited most gold exports (Friedman and Schwartz 1963, p. 220).

The gold value of the pound therefore was fixed within a few percent of its traditional value until the fall of 1917, three years after the start of the war. It is true that a trader could not get gold directly from the Bank of England, but the Bank still intervened to preserve the value of the pound. A trader selling pounds therefore would end up with dollars that could be sold for gold. This procedure may have introduced additional transaction costs into the operation of the gold standard, but it left the basic operation intact.

After the United States prohibited gold exports, the Bank of England continued to stabilize the dollar–sterling exchange (Brown 1940, pp. 66–69). Therefore, even though the link to gold had been temporarily broken, the regime of fixed exchange rates continued. The exchange system was the gold standard (slightly damaged), not an alternative structure.[2]

The Cunliffe Committee appointed toward the end of the war to consider Britain's postwar monetary problems consequently assumed that the gold standard would continue in operation. The problems the committee faced were whether to re-establish the prewar par and how fast to do so. The committee's views were stated clearly at the start of its *First Interim Report*: "It is imperative that after the war the conditions necessary to the maintenance of an effective gold standard should be restored without delay." The alternative to the restoration of the prewar machinery was credit inflation, foreign gold drain, and jeopardy to Britain's trade position (Great Britain 1918, para. 1).

The principle was clear; its implementation was not. The British Gold and Silver (Export Control) Act of 1920 replaced the informal controls on gold exports that had proved effective during the war. The government abandoned its role as stabilizer of the pound–dollar exchange rate, and the act provided a five-year pass, allowing the pound to float through the postwar economic gyrations of the early 1920s (Brown 1940, pp. 184–186). But this act was like the wartime measures—a temporary expedient to buy time until the gold standard could be fully re-established. It represented a loss of control, not a loss of faith. This is apparent during the discussions held in 1924 to consider options on the expiration of the 1920 act.

Montagu Norman, governor of the Bank of England, strongly supported a return to prewar par, arguing that any sacrifice imposed on the economy by appreciation of the pound was in the cause of future prosperity. The reasoning was spelled out by one of the Bank's directors, Sir Charles Addis: "I think it would not be too high a price to pay for the substantial benefit of the trade of this country and its working classes, and also, although I put it last, for the recovery by the City of London of its former position as the world's financial center" (Moggridge 1972, pp.

41–42). Short-run loss would be offset by long-run gain to both industry and finance.

Benjamin Strong, governor of the New York Federal Reserve Bank, articulated the rest of this thought in a memo:

Mr. Norman's feelings, which, in fact, are shared by me, indicated that the alternative—failure of resumption of gold payments—being a confession by the British Government that it was impossible to resume, would be followed by a long period of unsettled conditions too serious really to contemplate. It would mean violent fluctuations in the exchanges, with probably progressive deterioration of the values of foreign currencies vis-à-vis the dollar; it would provide an incentive to all of those who were advancing novel ideas for nostrums and expedients other than the gold standard to sell their wares; and incentive to governments at times to undertake various types of paper money expedients and inflation; it might, indeed, result in the United States draining the world of gold with the effect that, after some attempt at some other mechanism for the regulation of credit and prices, some kind of monetary crisis would finally result in ultimate restoration of gold to its former position, but only after a period of hardship and suffering, and possibly some social and political disorder. (Strong Memorandum, January 11, 1925, quoted in Moggridge 1972, pp. 59–60)

Strong's lurid phrases expose the views current among monetary authorities of the twenties. He anticipated the Depression of the following decade but identified it as a consequence of abandoning gold instead of the result of attempting to preserve the gold standard. Strong could not even conceptualize any orderly alternatives to the gold standard. The only possible aftermath to economic and political chaos was the "ultimate restoration of gold."

It was not, then, that the gold standard was simply the best of a set of roughly comparable monetary arrangements. And it also was not a question with only minor effects on the economy. The alternatives to resumption were awful; it was worth some discomfort under the gold standard to avoid them. Every informed observer of the British economy of the mid-1920s acknowledged that there would be a cost to resumption. But the bankers thought that this was a small cost incurred to avoid a large one.

Norman clearly thought that the cost was quite small. He testified to that effect in 1924, and he reiterated the same view in 1930. He maintained that the impact of high Bank Rate was "more psychological than real," and he argued that the long-term interest rate was quite independent of Bank Rate except under unusually tight monetary stringency (Cairncross and Eichengreen 1983, p. 40). The costs of maintaining and operating the gold standard, in other words, were very slight, while the ills of abandoning it were great.

This view was tragically flawed. It slighted the interactions of financial and goods markets, and more important, it ignored the effect of resumption on British economic policy. Resumption sharply restricted the range of choices open to the British authorities. It subordinated care for the domestic market to action to preserve the gold standard. It conditioned the authorities to react to balance-of-payments deficits by contracting domestic activity. Even Keynes, who had opposed resumption in 1924, felt constrained after resumption to offer advice consistent with the maintenance of gold payments (Moggridge 1972, p. 1; Cairncross and Eichengreen 1983, p. 44).

In current terminology, the resumption of gold announced the continuation of the policy regime existing before the war. The most important implication of the British resumption in 1925 therefore was not the generally high Bank Rate it required. It was instead in the regime—the overall policy stance—reaffirmed by the government. It was this regime that put pressure on the world economy in the late 1920s and then dictated responses to events that were to prove disastrous. Keynes' apostasy shows the strength of the regime. Before the decision to resume the gold-standard regime, he could present a wide range of ideas; afterward, only suggestions within the regime would be heard.

The many investigators who have condemned the rate at which Britain resumed have ignored the distinction between actions and regimes. The return to $4.86 may or may not have been preferable to $4.50 or even $4.35.[3] But any of these rates were consistent with the regime of the gold standard. The level of the exchange rate may have determined the level of unemployment in the late 1920s and even the precise moment when the pound became embattled. But the gold-standard regime determined the structure of the macroeconomy. Even though—as I will describe later—exchange rates matter, the choice of $4.86 was largely the froth on the surface of the international economic currents (Brown 1940; Moggridge 1969; Moggridge 1972; Matthews 1986).

The distinction between actions and regimes is critical to an understanding of the Depression. First, it exposes the similarity between British decisions and actions in other countries. They were both expressions of a common regime, albeit in different circumstances. Second, the existence of the gold-standard regime makes comprehensible many seemingly random and perverse actions in the early 1930s. I will explore these implications in turn.

The British resumption in 1925 was not an isolated event. Britain had been the undisputed champion and manager of the gold standard before the war, and monetary authorities and private investors alike looked to London for guidance. The views that led to resumption were hardly restricted to Britain. Strong's views from America were echoed widely throughout Europe. The slow reestablishment of the gold standard in the 1920s was not the result of a dimming ardor for gold; it was the reflection of

the difficulty of operating the prewar standard in the post-war environment.

The United States had never fully gone off gold, and its adherence to the gold standard was even more steadfast than the British. There was little debate about the dollar's relation to gold because there was no problem that needed to be solved. But America's views were clear in its external relations. Since the United States emerged from the war in the strongest economic and financial shape, it was the primary lender to Europe. Maintenance of the gold (exchange) standard was an American condition for continuing to finance European reconstruction and growth. The "old fashioned religion," as Thomas Lamont described it, was exported with American capital (Maier 1975, pp. 589–590).

This is a familiar story. Every narrative of the 1920s recounts at some point the resumption of the gold standard under its modified name. But historians and economists assign very different weights to this development. Maier (1975), for example, discussed the gold standard only in the conclusion of his masterly account of European reconstruction. The gold standard functions in his account as an afterthought, an influence on events that is only part of the background. The gold standard needs to be brought into the foreground as a major decision made by postwar governments. Even though monetary regimes are a bit arcane to most historians—as they were to most politicians of the time—the continuation of the gold-standard regime was as important as the rates at which currencies were stabilized.

The choice of rates appeared natural for the United States and Britain, but not to France and Germany. The Genoa Conference, urged on by Norman, had endorsed the resumption of gold with devaluation for weak currencies, including France and (by implication) Germany

(Keynes 1922). This view has been attributed to Anglo-Saxon pride and racism (Silverman 1982, p. 58), but it seems more likely related to the continuing conflicts between and within these countries. Their struggle for European control had not ended with the cessation of hostilities. It was carried on in the Versailles Conference and reparations. The French occupation of the Ruhr in 1923 brought the continuing conflict back to a military level. The stabilization of the mark and the franc was not very far removed.

Germany responded to the occupation by accelerating its transition from inflation to hyperinflation. The Dawes Plan that resolved the crisis clearly aligned Germany with Britain and the United States. American capital would underwrite German stabilization. In return, Germany would return to the gold standard at prewar par. The Americans would remain a constant presence in Germany to enforce this condition (Schuker 1976; McNeil 1986).

France refused to accept the burden of deflation and—after a delay—stabilized the franc at one-fifth its prewar par. The French went on a *de facto* gold standard in December 1926, and on a *de jure* standard in June 1928. They jumped back on the gold-standard train at a favorable rate. Contemporaries and historians alike have been struck by the symmetry: the pound was overvalued and the franc undervalued in the late 1920s (Robbins 1934, p. 9; Schuker 1988).

The war had created what appeared to be a unique opportunity for some countries to change exchange rates. Under the gold standard countries were supposed to live with the exchange rate that history had bequeathed them, adjusting internally to it. But there was a recognition that at least some countries had been exempted from this requirement by the strains of the Great War. Britain and the United States, as the center of the gold standard and the

major country least affected by the war, were obligated to stand fast. But combatants like France and Germany—whose economies in the 1920s reflected the strains of ongoing conflict, carried out mostly by nonmilitary means—were allowed temporary freedom to choose their own rate. Germany lost this freedom in its hyperinflation; France used it to devalue the franc.

The rates were important, but the survival of the gold standard was even more momentous. Policymakers agreed that the gold values of currencies should be maintained and that gold should move easily between countries. The response to a shortage of reserves was to be deflation rather than devaluation. The response to a surfeit of gold was in theory inflation, but there were no penalties—at least none that singled out the creditor country—for non-compliance. This perhaps is the best meaning to give to the frequent judgment that the gold exchange standard was deflationary (Maier 1975, p. 589).

The gold standard then was fully reconstituted in 1925 or 1926. It was in trouble almost immediately. The British economy was plunged into social conflict, symbolized by the General Strike of 1926, over the allocation of the burden of a high pound. Robbins argued that this conflict then set in motion the boom and bust of the late 1920s. In 1927 the Federal Reserve "took the momentous decision of forcing a regime of cheap money" in order to support the struggling pound (by encouraging short-term capital movement into Britain and inflation in the United States that would increase British exports). Although low American interest rates may have initiated an expansion that in Robbins' words "got completely out of control," France—not Britain—was the beneficiary. The undervalued franc attracted gold like a magnet (Robbins 1934, pp. 52–54; Eichengreen 1986b).

Despite the Fed's efforts to help the hapless British, the Americans and the French accumulated gold and foreign exchange balances while Britain limped along. The asymmetry of the gold standard reveals the problem. The British economy had to be depressed to maintain gold payments; France and the United States did not have to expand. They did expand in the late 1920s; there were noteworthy booms in both countries. Did they expand enough to make the effects of the gold standard symmetric?

Clearly not. The two countries accumulated gold. They held 60 percent of the monetary gold by the end of the 1920s. That cannot have been the equilibrium distribution of gold. The two countries did not produce close to two-thirds of the world's production or generate two-thirds of its trade. This point can be made more precise. Eichengreen (1987) estimated a demand function for reserves for 24 countries for the period of the restored gold standard, 1929 to 1935. The demand for reserves in this function was a function of GNP, the import share, export variability, and money (taken to be endogenous). France and the United States stand out as having an excess demand for reserves. The United States held more almost three times the predicted amount of gold reserves; France, nearly five times as much.

These results support the traditional conclusion; France and the United States held excess gold reserves. I want to turn these results around, however, to suggest that the two countries had inadequately expanded their economies. Both countries needed to allow the money supply to expand more than they did. Fiscal expansion, not seriously contemplated in either country, would have reinforced the rise in demand.

The Eichengreen and Sachs (1986) model contains two identical countries, with familiar aggregate demand and supply curves. The interactions between the two countries are noted in three places. First, spending in each country,

the IS curve, depends on the relative prices of goods in the two countries. Changing exchange rates therefore reallocate demand between the two countries. Second, capital is assumed to flow easily between the two countries, so that interest rates are the same. Third, both countries are on the gold standard, and the money supply in each country is backed by gold. Gold movements in response to changing relative prices and capital movements then are reflected in the money supply. Changes in the money supply from other causes, of course, affect the other variables as well. The model is described more explicitly in appendix A.

This model therefore formalizes a simple view of the gold standard. It allows for changes in exchange rates—a prominent feature of the interwar period—and in monetary policies. In the Eichengreen and Sachs version it does not allow for fiscal or commercial policies. These extensions are discussed in appendix A. The model also lacks dynamics, which will be introduced in the next lecture. Even so, or perhaps because of its simplicity, this static model of the gold standard provides an illuminating framework for an overall view of the Depression.

Had France and the United States inflated, their excess gold holdings would have been reduced in several ways. Higher prices would have raised nominal income. The aim of policy, however, could not have been to cause relative prices to rise enough to justify the gold holdings in these countries. This was neither economically nor politically possible. Higher income also would have increased imports, presumably more than proportionately, raising the import share. Gold would have flowed out to pay for the higher imports, reducing the supply of reserves. The aim of policy should have been to encourage a more equitable distribution of gold between countries.

It might have been necessary for the United States and France to appreciate in order to effect this change. While it is hardly news to report that the French franc was under-valued, few commentators have said the same about the dollar. The more usual expression is that the pound was overvalued. I choose the less usual phrasing to emphasize that accommodation could have taken place on either the debtor or the creditor side of the gold ledger.

But the gold standard imposed no such discipline. In fact it removed revaluation from the policy arsenal after the im-mediate postwar reconstruction. France and the United States therefore had few tools with which to stem the in-flow of gold. They were free to sterilize the gold inflow and fight inflation in the late 1920s, which they did effectively. The burden of adjustment fell entirely on debtor countries. This burden was too great to bear in the context of the early 1930s. It destroyed the gold standard—along with a great deal else.

Eichengreen (1986a) recently offered a partial defense of the French to the charge of *willful* sterilization. Only open market operations by the Bank of France were capable of reducing the accumulation of gold; other possible actions would have had little effect. But the Bank of France was precluded from making open market purchases except under a few exceptional circumstances. It would have re-quired an act of Parliament to alter the Bank's charter for the Bank to avoid sterilization. This argument may absolve the Bank of France from the accusation of reckless self-interest, but it leaves the destabilizing role of the massive French gold holdings unchanged.

American gold holdings were larger than those of the French, and the American influence on events was larger. The ease of 1927 was replaced by increasingly contraction-ary actions in 1928 and 1929. Federal Reserve policy turned around at the start of 1928 to combat speculation in the New York stock market and to arrest the gold outflow started in part by the previous financial ease. The Fed's aim in the following two years was to curb speculation on the stock exchange while not depressing the economy. It failed on both counts (Wicker 1966, p. 123; Chandler 1971, pp. 83–87).

This policy did not impede stock-market speculation, but it reduced the rate of growth of monetary aggregates and caused the price level to turn down (Hamilton 1987). The monetary stringency was even tighter than it seems from examining the aggregate stock of money, because the demand for money to effect stock-market transactions rose, leaving less for other activities (Field 1984a; Field 1984b). Like France, the United States was not so much attempting to sterilize gold flows as it was responding to other influences—stock-market speculation in this case. The effect, however, was independent of intent.

The two countries with ample gold reserves were not expanding; the United States even was embarked on a deflationary policy. Countries with less adequate reserves could not be expected to supply expansionary force in opposition, and they did not. The British economy continued to limp along. The stock market boomed in 1928, but unemployment remained high. "Times were dull, and the outlook was never particularly promising" (Youngson 1960, p. 75).

The German economy was heavily dependent on capital imports in the 1920s (Holtfrerich 1986). Popular history regards the capital imports as a necessary offset to Germany's reparations payments; they were needed to solve the "transfer problem." The reality was quite different. Germany managed to avoid paying reparations by a variety of economic and political maneuvers that succeeded in postponing its obligations until they could be repudiated entirely. The capital inflow therefore represented a net increase in the resources available to the German economy. The gross capital inflow was over 5 percent of German

national income from 1919 to 1931; the net capital inflow
was over 2 percent (Schuker 1988, pp. 10–11).

Nevertheless, Hjalmar Schacht, president of the Reichsbank from 1923 to 1930, like his counterparts in the United
States, was worried about stock-market speculation. He
therefore undertook to discourage the inflow of capital. He
withdrew the tax exemption of foreign holders of German
bonds in December 1926, effectively eliminating foreign
flotation of German bonds during the first half of 1927. The
Reichsbank forced commercial banks to reduce discount-
ing by threatening to refuse to discount any bills from non-
cooperative banks. These actions were more severe than
those undertaken by the Federal Reserve in 1928, and they
had more visible effects. The German stock market crashed
in May 1927. This in turn led to an outflow of short-term
capital, which Schacht countered by raising the discount
rate and restoring the tax exemption for foreign bond-
holders. Foreign lending resumed, but at higher rates
(Balderston 1983).

German investors also demanded a risk premium for
government securities. The memory of the hyperinflation
hung heavily over the German economy. The Reichsbank's
limited control over the banking system was worrisome.
Workers demanded higher wages to protect themselves.
Various levels of the German government were investing
heavily. Further government expansion was suspect (Balderston 1982).

The primary explanation for the tightness of German
capital markets toward the end of the 1920s consequently
was German. But the German difficulties took place in the
context of contractionary policies in the other major industrial countries as well. The effects of German actions therefore were magnified by external conditions. The price of
German bonds in New York fell both because of Schacht's

actions and because the Federal Reserve was increasing interest rates in New York.

The Atlantic economy, in other words, was in the grip of deflationary policies at the end of the 1920s. Each national story differs, but they were all reflections of an underlying theme. The gold standard had been revived, but the conditions that had sustained it before the war no longer existed. The pound was overvalued; the franc, undervalued. Both the Americans and the Germans were trying to stamp out "speculation." The result was that government policies everywhere were set to discourage economic activity.

Predictably, they did. American industrial production reached a peak in mid-1929, and the stock market crashed in September. The German economy was already declining, and the depression spread. The question then is what turned the decline into the Great Depression?

The answer, at least in the United States, has been dominated by the discussion of specific events. Friedman and Schwartz isolated the bank failures in December 1930, as the pivotal event, and debate has swirled around that "cause" (Friedman and Schwartz 1963; Temin 1976; Bernanke 1983). I think this emphasis is misplaced. The issue is not any specific action, but the policy regime within which actions took place. Government economic policies were consistently deflationary in the early 1930s, pushing the world economy ever downward.

Germany and the United States experienced the worst of the Depression, as can be seen in figure 1.1. Historical analysis rightly has centered on them. Curiously, the German debate is largely about fiscal policy, while the American debate rages about monetary policy. This difference is understandable in terms of the intellectual history of the two countries. The overriding issue in Germany is the growth of Nazi power, and it therefore is natural to focus on the policies of successive parliamentary governments. The more placid history of the United States has allowed a focus on narrower issues—in this case, whether monetary or fiscal policies are the best tools for stabilizing the economy.

This explanation for the difference between American and German scholarship poses a problem. If indeed the contrast is due to the intellectual traditions in the two nations, is there any reason to think that it also reflects a difference in the underlying history? I think not. Each national story looks at one part of the same elephant; it is necessary here to draw a more complete picture.

It is no secret that the Federal Reserve pursued a deflationary policy in the early 1930s. It also is true that the Federal Reserve had been crafted to be independent of the federal administration. I want to argue, however, that Federal Reserve policy was part of a general governmental policy of deflation. It was not an artifact of the structure or personalities of the Federal Reserve System itself; it represented one aspect of a unitary national policy.

President Hoover wanted to promote recovery almost from the beginning of the Depression. Hardly a traditional conservative, he still was limited by his view of the proper role of government. The government, as he saw it, should guide the private economy only by encouraging efficiency and cooperation between government and industry. But the government need not and should not encroach on the functions of the private economy. The prevailing view was that the economy would equilibrate itself after a shock. Recent history—the business cycles of the first three decades of the twentieth century—confirmed that view (Stein 1969, ch. 2; Barber 1985).

Although not spelled out by Hoover—who was not in the business of articulating economic theories—this policy stance derives from the same view of the economy as the gold standard. What is the mechanism that makes the economy self-correcting? The gold standard. A depressed economy would import less, acquire gold, and reflate. One role for government in this was to keep the burden of depression from falling too heavily on the workers. Hoover, opposed to direct government spending, discouraged wage cutting in 1921 and again in 1930. This was consistent with his support for high wages at all times to promote efficiency, expand demand, and reduce social tension (as well as union attractiveness).

The tone of government policy (due to Hoover's public reticence) as well as the substance of fiscal policy was set by Secretary of the Treasury Andrew Mellon, whose policy was to "liquidate labor, liquidate stocks, liquidate the farmers, liquidate real estate" (Hoover 1952, p. 30). Hoover therefore was very active, but primarily in attempting to cajole business leaders and state governments into action.

Hoover recommended a tax cut in December 1929, but not as a response to the nascent depression. Planning had started in the previous summer, at the height of the boom, and the tax reduction was a reaction to the growth of government revenues during the boom rather than the fall of production thereafter. It was in fact a reflection of balanced-budget ideology, not Keynesian demand management (Barber 1985, p. 85).

Despite the tax reduction and some increase in government spending, the fiscal stance of the government did not change between 1929 and 1930. The full-employment budget only expanded aggregate demand by 0.3 percent of GNP (Peppers 1973).[4] This set the pattern for the next few years. During the downturn fiscal policy typically was no more expansive than it had been at the peak of the boom.

There was one notable exception to this rule, an exception that proves (tests) the rule. The full-employment budget was considerably more expansive in 1931 than in any other year of the Depression. According to Brown (1956), it expanded demand by a full 2 percent of GNP more than the 1929 budget. This was not huge, considering the rapid fall in income between those two years. It was, however, large relative to the size of the government in the economy (4 percent of GNP).

The government budget was in deficit in 1931 because Congress passed a bill allowing veterans to borrow against a pension fund that had been established in 1925. This was strenuously opposed by Hoover, who characterized it as a "breach of fundamental principle." Secretary of the Treasury Mellon admitted that the funds might stimulate demand. In his words, "This would unquestionably have a stimulating effect on business, but it would be temporary stimulation of an artificial character and could hardly be expected to have such lasting qualities as would bring about a permanent recovery." In fact the Treasury borrowing needed to finance the veterans' bonus would crowd out private investment, providing little or no net stimulus. The Veterans' Bonus Bill of 1931 was passed over Hoover's veto (Barber 1985, pp. 108–111).[5]

The fiscal authorities felt themselves constrained to take no expansionary actions as the economy contracted in the early 1930s. The example of the veterans' bonus reveals the depth of their opposition; the bonus was handed to them without political risk and with a rationale that allowed the Hoover administration to maintain its ideological purity. Hoover, Mellon, and their associates declined the offer, fighting any fiscal expansion.

Both monetary and fiscal policy were contractionary in the early 1930s; no move was made to help the economy. The ideological link between this stance and the gold standard has been described in the context of fiscal policy. A more direct link can be shown in the conduct of monetary policy. The Federal Reserve had a clear choice in September 1931. The European monetary crisis had reached the United States. Britain had gone off gold. The United States could have followed the British lead and abandoned the gold standard, or—as it chose—it could have provided the traditional gold-standard response.

The Fed raised the discount rate and saved the dollar. The resulting rise in interest rates had a depressing effect on production as is clearly visible in figure 1.1. The Fed had contracted in the prosperous conditions of 1928 to stop a gold outflow; it did the same in the depressed climate of 1931. Adherence to the gold standard compelled the Federal Reserve to depress the economy further in the midst of the Great Depression.

German history reveals an almost identical pattern. Successive German governments refused to undertake expansionary action, clinging to the gold standard with as much tenacity as the American government. The Reichsbank also was contractionary, as noted already. And there were, in addition, special German incentives to contract that reinforced this posture.

The political economy of Weimar Germany was dominated by an inability to resolve the tensions in Weimar society. Reparations were used actively to distract attention from the underlying conflicts and externalize the problem. Germany made only one full reparations payment before refusing to pay more at the end of 1922. At the same time Germany induced a massive capital inflow through the inflationary reduction in the value of its foreign debt (Schuker 1988, pp. 14–23). Despite the absence of real burden from reparations, the German refusal to pay precipitated the French occupation of the Ruhr. Hyperinflation, already in process, rose to catastrophic heights.

The Dawes Plan that underwrote the German stabilization program remained a potent political and economic factor for Germany for the five years of its life. The Dawes loan was heavily oversubscribed in New York, and subsequent German loans sold well in America as well. But the

gain of stabilization was offset by ongoing obligations imposed by the Dawes Plan. In particular, Germany was
committed to stay on the gold standard, to maintain
adequate reserves, and to not devalue. To accomplish
these goals, German monetary policy had to be deflationary in the late 1920s (Hardach 1980; Schuker 1988, p. 27).
The burden of reparations was made palpable by the
presence in Berlin of a young, arrogant, non-German-
speaking agent general for reparations, S. Parker Gilbert
(McNeil 1986, pp. 27–30).

Despite the nominal obligation of reparations, Germany
had a deficit on current account in every year from 1924
through 1929 (Temin 1976, p. 154). In other words, Germans imported more goods and services than they sent
abroad. Reparations had no direct effect on the German
economy. In a different world Germany's leaders might
have resolved that they could live with this temporarily
benign condition. The Reagan administration in the United
States clearly decided that it could live for many years
in the 1980s with budget and trade deficits that were un-
thinkable to earlier governments. Weimar Germany, by
contrast, struggled ceaselessly for the reduction and
elimination of its reparations obligations (Hardach 1980;
1986; McNeil 1986; Schuker 1988).

The German government struggled, however, within
the confines of the rules of orthodox finance, that is, the
gold standard. As the downturn began due to the combination of American and German policies already described, the German authorities responded to their
external difficulties by depressing their internal economy. Schacht, president of the Reichsbank until March
1930 and chief German negotiator for the Young Plan,
had consistently pursued a deflationary strategy. Hans
Luther, his successor at the Reichsbank, followed suit,

keeping the discount rate well above the rates in London and New York in attempt to reduce the bank's continuing loss of gold (Northrop 1938, pp. 297–300).

The fiscal authorities were even more aggressive in their deflationary efforts. The move toward highly restrictive government budgets came at the beginning of 1930. Heinrich Brüning, chancellor from March 1930 to May 1932, continued this policy, relentlessly attempting to deflate the economy to restore equilibrium in the manner of the gold standard. Germany, unable to pay its foreign bills at gold par, had to reduce internal prices until it could. With a series of austerity decrees and an attempt to legislate price cuts directly, the "iron chancellor" exerted a constant downward pressure on the German economy. The government deficit *decreased* in the early 1930s, even as the economy declined: expenditures and transfers fell even faster than tax revenues, exerting deflationary pressure on the economy (James 1986, pp. 52–60).

Only in Britain was another policy route chosen. The Bank of England had hewn to a restrictive policy since 1925 in defense of the overvalued pound. Interest rates were kept high to attract short-term capital and to stabilize the pound. They also had a depressing effect on domestic economic activity, despite Norman's well-known assertions to the contrary. When pressure on the pound increased in mid-1931, however, the Bank refused to raise Bank Rate dramatically because of its internal effects. O.M.W. Sprague, an American advisor to the Bank of England, urged it to raise Bank Rate to punitive levels. The Bank refused (Sayers 1976, p. 405n). Instead, French and American credits were spent in defense of the pound. The Labor government also resisted pressure for cuts in unemployment benefits, moderating the fiscal contraction. The limited measures undertaken by the British monetary and fiscal authorities were insufficient to sustain the value of the pound. Unwilling to impose the draconian measures employed in Germany, the British abandoned the gold standard on September 20, 1931 (Cairncross and Eichengreen 1983; Kunz 1987).

The British therefore were both the champions of the revived gold standard in the 1920s and of its abandonment in the 1930s. Unfortunately, other countries were not as agile in their policy shifts. The United States held onto gold until 1933, France until 1936, and Germany—subject to more than the usual constraints in the early 1930s—throughout the decade.

In the static equilibrium model of international linkages, this devaluation clearly helped the British economy. It lowered British export prices relative to foreign, and it allowed Britain to establish—after an unnecessary half-year delay—a relatively permissive monetary policy. The effect on the rest of the world was not so beneficial. According to the model, devaluation does not beggar the neighbors if gold flows out from the devaluing country, allowing monetary expansion elsewhere to offset the effects of the relative price change (Eichengreen and Sachs 1985). But the newly liberated Britain did not allow gold to flow out. The Bank of England took the opportunity to build up its reserves (Howson 1980, pp. 4–6). The effect of Britain's action on the rest of the world therefore was deflationary. The British devaluation nonetheless was a step in the right direction. Had the other major countries followed suit, the effect would have been expansionary.

The effects of the devaluation in Britain can be seen in figures 1.1 and 1.2. The British economy did not recover from its long-term doldrums, but it also did not follow the American and German economies down into the abyss. Britain decoupled its fortunes from the countries adhering to the gold standard and allowed policy to become less restrictive. The result was an unusually mild depression in

Britain. The paradox is that the country most identified with the reconstitution of the gold standard after the First World War was the first to abandon it also.

More extended analysis of the Depression's propagation is reserved to the next lecture. Enough has been revealed here, however, to suggest some conclusions of interest. I will divide them into three groups: historical implications, theoretical implications, and modern parallels.

The Great Depression was caused, I am arguing, by the strains of the First World War on the gold standard. The war itself led to the suspension of the gold standard, but not—as is widely stated—to its demise. The system was revived after the war in essentially its prewar form. Conditions were very different, making restoration of the gold standard arduous. It therefore required intense attachment to the gold standard to complete its restoration.

The combination of changed conditions and some policy choices of the 1920s—notably the choice of values for the pound and the franc—created great strains in the operation of the interwar gold standard. The asymmetry of the gold standard forced countries lacking reserves to contract more than reserve-rich countries expanded. Gold-standard rules dictated deflation rather than devaluation for the former. The result was a world deflationary policy in the late 1920s.

The instability of the interwar gold standard was the effect of the First World War, but the Depression was not the inevitable result of the war. Had economic planners absorbed the lesson that the institutions of the Edwardian era were no longer viable, postwar history might have been far different. It was the combination of the shock of the First World War, an unchanging international institution, and an unyielding policy regime that generated the Great Depression.

The Depression was not even inevitable in 1929. Had policymakers been able to free themselves from the strait-jacket of the gold standard, they could have instituted countercyclical policies. But without that change, the rules of the gold standard mandated deflation. Policies designed to effect deflation magnified the deflationary forces present in 1929. Holding the industrial economies to the gold-standard last was about the worst thing that could have been done.

This view of the Depression answers questions implicit in some other interpretations. Lewis (1949, p. 52) argued that the Depression was caused by events in America. Friedman and Schwartz (1963) agreed and paid only the most cursory attention to the interaction of the industrial economies, drawing their main conclusion on the American role from the flow of gold to the United States. This part of their discussion has been criticized (Fremling 1985), but their identification of the Depression as an American event has won wide acceptance. How then to understand the events in Europe at the end of the 1920s?

I argued in my earlier work for an independent influence from Germany (Temin 1971, 1976). The specifics of that demonstration have been undermined by new data (Balderston 1977, 1983). But the thrust of the argument stands. The Depression drew its force from the deflation-ary policies of both the United States and Germany. These two economies interacted with each other and with influences from other countries to make the Depression a unique historical event. It was the international ad-herence to the rules of classical economy that led to the worldwide Depression.

Friedman and Schwartz also represented the Depression as the result of a tiny cause on a highly unstable system. They argued "that small events at times have large con-sequences." In particular, they asserted that the cause of the Depression was the untimely 1928 death of Benjamin Strong, president of the Federal Reserve Bank of New York. As they recognized, this statement of cause—of impulse in modern terminology—implies a magnifying propagation mechanism, "chain reactions and cumulative forces," in their words (Friedman and Schwartz 1965, p. 123).

The death of Strong was a minor event in the history of the Great Depression. Although he was an able and articulate central banker, he died in 1928, at the height of the revived gold standard. He was, as we have seen, a passionate believer in the gold standard. Nothing had happened at the time of his death to shake that view. There is no evidence that he would have been more able than anyone else to break out of the gold-standard train of thought. The Great Depression was the result of a much larger deflationary impulse.

In fact one of the problems with modern views of the Depression has been an absence of causes. Rejecting Friedman and Schwartz's rather special view has seemed to leave a void (Temin 1976). Putative propagating mechanisms have proliferated, but eligible causes have not. The First World War always appears in the historical literature, but without an explanation for the long delay between war and depression. This story reinstates the Great War as the deflationary impulse that caused the Great Depression and provides a mechanism for its long gestation.

Kindleberger has argued that the First World War destabilized the international economy by eliminating London as its clear financial center. The dual leadership of Britain and the United States proved unstable; the Depression was caused by the absence of a clear hegemonic power. The central bank in a hegemonic economy would have been able to provide the relief to ailing economies that would have obviated the Depression (Kindleberger 1986).

Kindleberger's view contains an implicit assumption. He assumed that the hegemon would have acted to stabilize the international monetary system. He looked back to the prewar economy and took the Bank of England as a model. Had an institution with the Bank's power existed in 1930, it would have been able to maintain at least an approximation to prosperity.

I think that this assumption is wrong. The inference from earlier years assumes a system that could be easily stabilized. I have argued here that the interwar economy suffered from a major shock that had been systematically ignored in the recreation of prewar monetary arrangements. The central banks were part of the problem in this story. Each of them acted in concert with its government and in accord with common views, although not as part of explicit cooperation (except for Germany under the Dawes Plan), and they therefore moved in the same direction. They all adopted deflationary policies.

For Kindleberger's argument to hold, there must both have been a single hegemonic central bank and actions by this bank that differed from the actions of any central bank of the time. There is no evidence that the historical candidates for this position would have acted in this way. The Bank of France and the Federal Reserve were turned inward to their own economies. Neither bank could even make open market purchases to help their own economies; it is hard to envision them extending to Germany and Britain the massive loans that would have been needed to shore up their currencies in the conditions of the early 1930s. It is even harder to think of the Fed breaking out of the ideology shared by all of the central banks with which it was in contact and abandoning the constraints of the gold standard at a time when America's reserves were not under pressure.[6]

The Bank of England acted better. It left gold early in the Depression. This action was taken, however, out of weakness, not out of strength. It is only with hindsight and modern analysis that we judge it positively. It was widely seen at the time and has been generally seen since as a failure of British policy. Given the record of the Bank in re-establishing the prewar gold parity of the pound, there is little evidence that, given the power, it would have acted with the requisite boldness.

It is always possible that any of these banks would have grown into the role of central bank to the world. If one of these countries, presumably the United States, had emerged from the First World War as the clear center of the world economy, it might have come to understand that world economic conditions had been fundamentally altered by the war and that the prewar gold standard was a treacherous tool. But then, as Kindleberger always asked his students, if my grandmother had wheels, would she be a wheelbarrow?

The primary theoretical implication of this story is that macroeconomic policy matters. There is a school of thought that has denied the ability of policymakers to affect economic events (Sargent and Wallace 1975). This simply is not true. The Depression was the result of policies taken by national governments and central banks. The concord of these bodies has blinded observers to the presence of volition in these acts.

I have traced the common policy stance of the major economic powers back to the years just after the First World War. The attempt to reconstitute the *status quo ante* by reviving the gold standard was a dreadful mistake. But it was a decision of men who could have chosen differently. The men in question were, to be sure, prisoners of their ideology, and it would have been hard to tread a different path. Difficult, but not impossible. The British pound, for example, floated for five years after the conclusion of the war.

There was ample time and evidence in that time to think of alternative international financial arrangements.

It was harder to break out of the gold-standard framework a decade later, after herculean efforts had been put into its restoration. On the other hand, the costs of adhering to this standard also rose as the world economy began to see the effects of the deflationary policies of the previous decade. The example of Britain again shows that it was not impossible to make a different choice. Yet the United States, Germany, and France continued to impose deflationary policies for three long years in the midst of the world's greatest depression.

The view I am presenting here reverses a traditional conclusion of international economics. Contemporary observers drew from the interwar experience the conclusion that floating exchange rates lead to economic chaos (Nurkse 1944). They correctly observed the correlation, but they reversed the causation. It was actually that economic instability leads to floating exchange rates. It was impossible to maintain the gold standard in the interwar period.

In fact it was the attempt to preserve the gold standard that produced the Great Depression. These attempts imposed deflationary forces on the world economy that were unprecedented in their strength and worldwide consistency. These deflationary forces were maintained long enough to cause an unprecedented interruption in economic activity. When the attempt to preserve the gold standard finally failed, alternative monetary arrangements were put together in the worst possible conditions. To blame the new system for these conditions is to blame the messenger, not to identify the cause of distress.

We therefore should be a bit humble in our approach to macroeconomic policy. The economic authorities of the late 1920s had no doubt that their model of the economy was correct. Benjamin Strong articulated in 1925 the dangers to be anticipated from abandoning the gold standard. He did not see that these were the dangers of *maintaining* this system. It is not given to us to know how future generations will understand the economic relations that govern how we live. We should strive to be open to alternative interpretations of current events, on the ground that our greatest fears may be attached to the wrong policies. More specifically, we should be wary of policies that steadfastly ignore changes in the world economy, policies suited for conditions of some bygone time.

How likely are we to experience such an outmoded regime? The new Bush administration seems poised to exhibit just such an obsolete regime. There was no discussion of the overriding economic problems of the United States in the 1988 electoral campaign. There has been no serious recognition that the United States has gone from the world's largest creditor to the world's largest debtor in less than a decade. There has been only token appreciation of the great imbalances in international trade. It would be dangerous—but by no means surprising—if President Bush followed policies appropriate to a time when the United States had more economic power and more freedom of economic maneuver than it possesses today.

Such solipsistic actions could jeopardize world economic health, as they did just about a decade ago, in the great monetarist experiment. In the face of rising inflation, coming both from the Vietnam War and the two oil shocks, President Jimmy Carter appointed Paul Volcker to be chairman of the Board of Governors of the Federal Reserve in 1979. Volcker initiated a monetarist policy process in which the quantity of money was used as an index of monetary policy in place of the traditional interest rates. This policy, adopted in the fall of 1979, was in fact a sharply deflationary one, designed to wring inflation out of the economy.

The growth of real GNP in the United States ground to a halt for three years. Industrial production fell over 10 percent from its peak in the summer of 1981 and real GNP by 3 percent. Unemployment rose steadily, peaking at over 10 percent at the end of 1982. Inflation also went down, making the policy a success in some quarters, but at the cost of the deepest recession since the Great Depression (Citibank 1988).

By the summer of 1982, after three years of deflationary policy, the world economy was in sad shape. Britain under Margaret Thatcher had adopted a similar stance with similar effects. Other countries had been drawn as well into the American deflation. Less developed countries in particular were in desperate straits: demand for their products was down, the cost of imported oil was up, and the supply of foreign capital dried up. The international debt crisis threatened to explode.

There was at that time, I think, the possibility of an economic meltdown. Had the deflationary policy been continued for another six months, financial collapses and fiscal distress might have created conditions that would have continued and even accelerated the downturn. In the recent words of Frank Morris, the retired president of the Boston Federal Reserve Bank, "God knows what kind of depression we would have seen if we had pursued policy with monetarist zeal in the summer of 1982" (Warsh 1988, p. 88).

Fortunately, Volcker's policy did not recreate the Great Depression. He abandoned his deflationary regime in July 1982. I will describe in the next lecture what happens when monetary and fiscal authorities maintain such a regime through thick and thin.

# 2      The Midas Touch: The Spread of the Great Depression

I argued in the first lecture that the First World War was the impulse that led to the Great Depression. This solved one problem at the cost of creating another. The shock in this view was commensurate with the effect. There is no need to hypothesize an instability so great as to destroy the world economy in response to a small shock. Offsetting this desirable attribute of the argument, however, is the necessity to explain why a shock in 1914–18 produced a depression in 1929–33.

To explain this delayed reaction, the discussion in the first lecture had to initiate the discussion of propagation. I argued that the gold standard was the primary propagation mechanism. Despite the conventional view to the contrary, the gold standard was not "swept away in a few days by the financial tides accompanying the onset of World War I" (Dam 1982, p. 19). Gold payments were stopped, and exchange rates floated. But this had happened before; it was the way gold-standard countries coped with short-term pressures. This suspension involved Britain instead of the United States, as had been typical of the previous decades. Nevertheless, this was a reflection of grave problems, not the end of the whole system.

The vitality of the gold standard is shown in the general agreement at the end of the war that prewar gold parities needed to be re-established. It was not simply that regular gold exports had to be revived, but that they should be allowed at the same price as before. Although not possible for all countries, the prewar parities provided a point of departure for even those currencies not returning to the prewar par.

The postwar gold standard spread the shock of the war in two ways, by imparting a deflationary bias to national economic policies of gold-standard countries in the late 1920s and by indicating that deflation was the appropriate remedy for the ills of the early 1930s. The first tendency created the conditions for the Depression throughout the 1920s. The second pattern directed national economic policies in ways that accentuated the economic decline.

Only the first of these two channels was detailed in the first lecture. The conditions of the late 1920s were described, and I argued that the deflationary policies in the United States, Germany, and Britain, coupled with the sterilization of gold in France, were more than sufficient to initiate the Great Depression. It is time now to turn to the economic decline, to show how the policies of governments interacted with the decisions of individuals to create the Great Depression.

It will prove convenient to divide the period at the European financial crisis. This yields two phases of the Depression: the initial decline from mid-1929 to mid-1931, and its continuation from mid-1931 to mid-1933. The literature on America has concentrated on the first of these subperiods; works on Germany have tended to focus on the second. I will attempt to unify the treatment of the two phases.

Industrial production began to decline in 1928 in Germany and in 1929 in the United States. As described in

lecture 1, these declines were the natural result of the contractionary policies undertaken by the governments of
these countries. The Germans were worried about foreign
lending and reparations, the Americans were upset about
domestic speculation. The preferred cure for both ills was
the same: restrict access to credit. The resulting tightness
of credit, beginning at the end of the 1920s and continuing
into the early 1930s in Europe, was severe enough to explain the fall in production and prices during the first
phase of the Depression.

The American economy also experienced a fall in consumption in 1930 that was too large to be explained easily
(Temin 1976). This autonomous fall in consumption was
denied by Mayer (1980) and revived by Hall (1986). It is still
an important part of the American story.

Four events from the fall of 1929 to the end of 1930 have
been accorded prominent roles in the propagation of the
Depression. Since research on this first phase of the Depression has concentrated on the United States, at least
three of them concern events in America. The four events
are the stock-market crash in New York, the Smoot-
Hawley tariff of 1930, the so-called first banking crisis of
Friedman and Schwartz, and the worldwide collapse of
commodity prices. Even the last of these, though worldwide, probably had its origin in the United States. It is
distinguished from the other three events by being an
important part of the propagation mechanism.

Time has not been kind to the school of thought that
blames the Depression on the stock-market crash (Galbraith 1961). The stock market has gone up and down
many times since then without producing a similar movement in income. The most obvious parallel was in the fall
of 1987. The isomorphism was uncanny. The stock market
fell almost exactly the same amount on almost exactly the
same dates. (So much for those who think seasonality is a

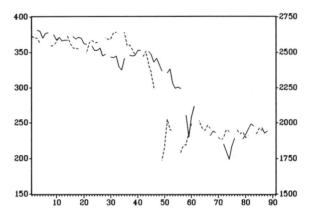

**Figure 2.1**
The daily Dow Jones Average, September–November, 1929 and
1987. *Solid line*: 1929 (left scale); *dotted line*: 1987 (right scale).
Sources: Pierce (1986); New York Stock Exchange (1987).

phenomenon of the past.) Shown in figure 2.1 are stock
prices on the same dates in 1929 and 1987.

If the crash of 1929 was an important independent shock
to the economy, then the crash of 1987 should have been
equally disastrous. The stock market had grown in the in-
tervening half century, and news of the stock market was
pervasive. Many more people owned stocks in 1987, even
though stocks probably were a smaller part of personal
wealth than in 1929. There were strains on the international economy to rival those of the 1920s, centering on American rather than German borrowing. And stock markets
around the world were much more closely synchronized in
1987 than in the late 1920s.

Despite a flurry of speculation in the popular press, the
world economy did not turn down in the fall of 1987. The
boom in production that had been under way for five years
continued apace. It follows that a stock-market crash is not
a big enough event on its own to initiate a depression.

The two crashes reflected changes in interest rates and expectations, albeit imperfectly. The value of a capital asset is determined by the discounted present value of expected future earnings and payments. This value changes when the interest rate varies, falling when the interest rate rises. Interest rates were rising in the fall of both 1929 and 1987, and this undoubtedly had an effect on stock prices. Changes in the expected future earnings, however, were more important. Investors lost faith in the continuation of the boom; they readjusted their expectations downward. Shiller (1981) has shown that stock prices move far more than can be explained by subsequent changes in dividends. It follows that movements of the stock market are only fair measures of expectations. The two crashes are not yet fully understood.[7]

In neither case was the change cataclysmic. Stocks retained the major part of their values after each crash. The effects of the change in value therefore were minimal. The stock market crash in 1929 helped to communicate the Fed's tight monetary policy throughout the economy. But it was not a strong or independent force of its own. The crash of 1987 reflected nervousness about the Reagan fiscal policy but, like its earlier cousin, had little effect on expenditures.

That is not to say that the crash of 1929 had no effect. As a part of the propagation mechanism, the stock-market crash had several effects. It reduced private wealth by about 10 percent. It increased consumers' leverage, that is, the ratio of their debts to their assets. And it no doubt increased consumers' uncertainty about what the future would bring. Each of these effects tended to depress consumer expenditures, particularly the demand for consumer durables. None of these influences was large enough to explain the 1930 fall in consumption in isolation. They are nonetheless parts of the explanation (Temin 1976; Mishkin 1978; Romer 1988).

The idea that the Smoot-Hawley tariff was a major cause of the Depression is an enduring conviction. It was stated at the time, reiterated after the Second World War by Lewis (1949, pp. 59–61), and again more recently and more strongly by Meltzer (1976). It has found its way into popular discussion and general histories (Kennedy 1987, pp. 282–283). Despite its popularity, however, this argument fails on both theoretical and historical grounds.

A tariff, like a devaluation, is an expansionary policy. It diverts demand from foreign to home producers. It may thereby create inefficiencies, but this is a second-order effect. The Smoot-Hawley tariff also may have hurt countries that exported to the United States. The popular argument, however, is that the tariff caused the American Depression. The argument has to be that the tariff reduced the demand for American *exports* by inducing retaliatory foreign tariffs (Eichengreen 1989).

Exports were 7 percent of GNP in 1929. They fell by 1.5 percent of 1929 GNP in the next two years. Given the fall in world demand in these years from the causes described here, not all of this fall can be ascribed to retaliation from the Smoot-Hawley tariff. Even if it is, real GNP fell over 15 percent in these same years. With any reasonable multiplier, the fall in export demand can only be a small part of the story. And it needs to be offset by the rise in domestic demand from the tariff. Any net contractionary effect of the tariff was small (Dornbusch and Fischer 1986, pp. 466–470).

The primary propagating mechanism in the American Depression identified by Friedman and Schwartz revolved around banking panics. They identified the first of three banking crises in December 1930 with the failure of the Bank of United States. Had the banks responded to panic in the fashion of nineteenth-century restrictions of payments, they claimed, the Depression need never have happened. "By cutting the vicious circle set in train by the search for liquidity, restriction would almost certainly have prevented the subsequent wave of bank failures that were destined to come in 1931, 1932, and 1933, just as restriction in 1893 and 1907 had quickly ended bank suspensions arising primarily from lack of liquidity." But, Friedman and Schwartz continued, "the existence of the [Federal] Reserve System prevented concerted restriction" (Friedman and Schwartz 1963, p. 311).

The events after the restriction of payments in 1893 and 1907 show that the American economy of the time was very stable. A restriction of payments occurred when the banks no longer honored their commitment to exchange deposits for currency at par. When a single bank refused to redeem its obligations at par, it was insolvent. But when banks acted in concert, there was an effective devaluation, with a market price for deposits. The price was determined, like all prices, by the forces of supply and demand. People who were afraid that the price of deposits would decline from its level at any point in time wanted to sell, driving down the price. People who thought that the price of deposits had already fallen and was due to rise back toward par wanted to buy, driving up the price. The market price was where the supply from the former group just matched the demand from the latter. Table 2.1 shows the actual discounts on deposits in the aftermath of the two restriction. The discounts were both small and short-lived. The currency premium was never more than 4 percent; it had fallen to almost nothing in a month, even though full resumption came somewhat later. Most people, in other words, expected the banks to resume payments at par speedily. They did not anticipate a major depression or

**Table 2.1**
Daily currency premium, 1893, 1907
(percent)

| Date | 1893 | 1907 |
|------|------|------|
| 1 | NA | $2\frac{3}{4}$ |
| 2 | NA | $2\frac{1}{2}$ |
| 3 | $1\frac{3}{8}$ | NA |
| 4 | $\frac{3}{7}$ | $3\frac{1}{4}$ |
| 5 | $1\frac{1}{2}$ | NA |
| 6 | NA | 3 |
| 7 | 2 | $2\frac{7}{8}$ |
| 8 | $2\frac{1}{4}$ | $2\frac{1}{2}$ |
| 9 | $3\frac{1}{2}$ | $1\frac{1}{2}$ |
| 10 | 3 | NA |
| 11 | $1\frac{1}{2}$ | $2\frac{5}{8}$ |
| 12 | $1\frac{1}{2}$ | $3\frac{1}{2}$ |
| 13 | NA | $3\frac{1}{2}$ |
| 14 | 2 | $2\frac{1}{2}$ |
| 15 | 2 | $2\frac{1}{4}$ |
| 16 | 2 | 1 |
| 17 | $2\frac{1}{4}$ | NA |
| 18 | $2\frac{1}{2}$ | $2\frac{1}{2}$ |
| 19 | $3\frac{1}{2}$ | $1\frac{7}{8}$ |
| 20 | NA | $1\frac{1}{2}$ |
| 21 | $2\frac{1}{8}$ | 3 |
| 22 | 2 | $2\frac{1}{8}$ |
| 23 | $1\frac{1}{2}$ | $\frac{1}{2}$ |
| 24 | $1\frac{1}{2}$ | NA |
| 25 | $1\frac{1}{4}$ | $1\frac{3}{8}$ |
| 26 | $\frac{7}{8}$ | $1\frac{1}{8}$ |
| 27 | NA | $\frac{3}{8}$ |
| 28 | $\frac{1}{2}$ | NA |
| 29 | $\frac{3}{8}$ | $\frac{1}{4}$ |
| 30 | $\frac{1}{4}$ | |

Source: Sprague (1910), pp. 187, 280–281.
Note: The dates are the days of the first month of suspended payments, August in 1893 and November in 1907. (The premium was lower or zero thereafter.) The premiums shown are the averages of the maximum and the minimum premiums reported, whether for buying or selling. Missing observations represent Sundays and election day (November 5).

further bank crises. They did not rush to sell discounted deposits.

Friedman and Schwartz therefore adopted an inconsistent position toward the banking crisis of 1930. On the one hand, they said that the economy was unstable, that a small event set off the Great Depression. In fact they traced the cause of the Depression back to the death of Benjamin Strong in 1928, even though their main story starts with the banking crisis in 1930. On the other hand, they implied that the economy was very stable, that a restriction of payments would have resulted in only a tiny change in the price of deposits—like the 2 or 3 percent seen in 1893 and 1907—and that this change would have brought the economy back onto an even keel. They cannot have it both ways. Either there was an impulse more powerful than the death of the head of the New York Fed or the economy was far less stable in 1930 than in 1893 and 1907 (and a suspension of bank payments would have had only limited impact).

The effects of the banking failures in December 1930 have been a matter of some debate. Friedman and Schwartz argued that they reduced the supply of money by increasing the banks' demand for reserves and the public's demand for currency. This in turn depressed spending. The underlying model was a static one, like the Eichengreen and Sachs (1986) model underlying lecture 1.

The problem with this chain of reasoning is that the monetary restriction should have affected income through the financial markets. Even if the lowered demand for money in the Depression eventually led to low interest rates, we still should observe a rise in interest rates at the time of the banking crisis—before its effects had run their course. No such credit stringency is observed at the start of 1931 (Temin 1976; Wicker 1982).

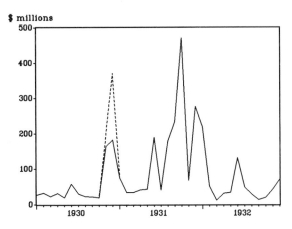

**$ millions**

**Figure 2.2**
Liabilities of failed banks, 1930–1932. *Solid line*: bank failures, excluding the Bank of United States and Caldwell & Co.; *dotted line*: all bank failures. Source: Bernanke (1983); Wicker (1980); Wigmore (1985, p. 125).

I now think that I should have gone further than I did a dozen years ago. The events of late 1930 do not merit the appellation that Friedman and Schwartz bestowed upon them. There was an increase in bank failures in November and December of 1930. But much of the rise was due to the failure of just two banks. Caldwell and Company failed in Tennessee, and the Bank of United States failed in New York City. Both of these banks had undergone reckless expansion in the late 1920s, and their overblown empires collapsed under the pressure of the emerging Depression.

It is instructive to subtract the liabilities of these two banks from the total liabilities in failed banks in those months. Even without allowing for the local ripple effect of Caldwell's failure that Wicker (1980) described, this operation alters the picture of bank failures. The new series is shown in figure 2.2, where the original series is given in dotted lines for comparison. (The major change is due to the omission of the Bank of United States; Caldwell and

Co. was small potatoes by comparison.) The rise in "other bank failures" was large, but not of the same scale as the rise in the summer and fall of 1931 (White 1984). The level of bank failures also returned to its earlier level at the end of 1930, where it stayed for four months. There was no reaction in the markets for short-term credit aside from a temporary rise in rates in Tennessee. The "first banking crisis" was a minor event in the history of the Great Depression.

This is revealed also by the behavior of the money supply. Despite the attention I and others gave to the effects of the "first banking crisis," the behavior of the money supply in the crisis has escaped critical attention until now. This was an important omission in the argument, for there was no fall in the stock of money at the end of 1930. There was no shock to the quantity of money that could have produced a large macroeconomic effect.

Instead, there was the beginning of a movement to increase currency in the hands of the public. This movement was small relative to the other events of the time. The change in the rate of growth of the money supply from the "banking crisis" therefore was swamped by changes from other causes. Even with the hindsight of history, statistical tests reject the hypotheses that the rate of decline of the money supply was altered by the "first banking crisis." As a result there was no reason to expect interest rates to react to such a change. (See appendix B and figure 2.4.)

Nevertheless, two alternative mechanisms have been proposed for the effects of the banking crisis. Schwartz asserted that the the price of money was not the interest rate. It was instead the inverse of the price level. By focusing exclusively on the price of goods, she assumed that an excess demand for money would have resulted in people selling *only* goods to acquire money, driving down their price. Interest rates would have been unaffected. This is

hardly an accurate description of the interwar economy. To restore money balances, people would have sold their most liquid assets, which were financial rather than real. Even if they sold all their assets in proportion, the excess demand for money would have driven down the price of financial assets, raising the interest rate. Schwartz's mechanism does not provide a propagation path independent of interest rates (Schwartz 1981; Temin 1981).

Bernanke proposed a different explanation. He argued that the effect of banking panics operated through credit rationing. Credit became harder to get for many borrowing firms, who had to shop around for loans or do without. Published interest rates did not reflect this added cost because they were the cost of loans granted, not loans refused (Bernanke 1983).

Bernanke introduced a new concept, the cost of credit intermediation. He argued that banks were the low-cost intermediaries, collecting money from potential lenders and evaluating the risks of individual borrowers. Any lender had imperfect knowledge of the comparative risks of different firms. Banks specialized in making the best use of the available data. They acquired most of the loan business because they were the low-cost intermediaries. When banks failed, failed banks no longer could extend credit, and other banks switched into more liquid loans to protect themselves. This reduced the supply of the most efficient intermediation services and raised its cost and consequently the cost of loans to borrowers. Most affected were "households, farmers, unincorporated businesses, and small corporations."[8]

The hypothesized rise in the cost of credit intermediation had both aggregate supply and demand effects. Bernanke discounted the former on the grounds that "most larger corporations entered the decade with sufficient cash and liquid reserves to finance operations and any desired

expansion." He emphasized instead the intertemporal substitution effect of purchasers induced by the higher cost of borrowing. The cost of borrowing to small debtors is of course not observed. It is assumed equal to the observed rate on safe loans (to large firms and the government) plus a premium for credit intermediation that rose with bank failures. The published rate might not rise at all if banks feared that higher rates would attract riskier borrowers and projects (Stiglitz and Weiss 1981).

Bernanke tested this hypothesis by time-series regressions explaining the movements of industrial production. Although impressive, the evidence does not directly show the effects of the cost of credit intermediation. It is a sort of reduced form, demonstrating that bank failures and other proxies for risk were closely related to the drop in industrial production. This kind of test lacks the power to discriminate among competing hypotheses about propagating mechanisms in the Depression (Temin 1976).

A more direct test examines the progress of different industries. Bernanke noted explicitly that the rising cost of credit intermediation hurt households and small firms much more than large firms. Bank failures then should have hurt industries populated by family firms and other small businesses more than those composed of large, well-established firms. This view can be tested by comparing industries with large firms to those with small firms.

The test therefore is a cross-sectional, not a time-series, test. The fall in production in different two-digit industries is related to the characteristics of firms in those industries. The industries are characterized both by concentration ratios and by the incidence of identifiable large firms. In both cases the presence of large firms is *positively* related to the fall in production, not negatively as Bernanke's model predicts. Comparison with 1937–38 reveals that the cross-sectional pattern of industrial decline in the Great Depres-

sion was not unusual. Despite the banking crises the pattern of industrial decline—as opposed to its magnitude and duration—was unexceptional (see appendix B). Bernanke's model therefore must be rejected as a mechanism by which the banking failures decreased aggregate demand. The role of the "first banking crisis" is hard to see.

We need to take care here not to throw the baby out with the bath water. The American financial system was being battered at the end of the 1920s by the stock-market decline, business failures, bank failures, and international events. After the stock-market crash, firms shifted their new offerings from stocks to bonds. Net new stock offerings fell by $2.5 billion from 1929 to 1930, while net new bond offerings rose by $1.4 billion (Federal Reserve System 1943, p. 487; Temin 1976, p. 133). The price of lower grade industrial bonds then began to decline in late 1930. The increased supply of bonds lowered their price. Business and bank failures decreased the demand for bonds by increasing their perceived risk.[9]

A gap opened up between the cost of bank loans to firms that could borrow at the prime rate (falling steadily in 1929 and 1930) and the cost of industrial bonds for smaller firms. This is the kind of premium that Bernanke was talking about, although market prices reflected this premium rather well. In fact, since bonds were being reclassified to show their increased risk at this time, the return on risky bonds was rising for two reasons: bonds of a given riskiness were worth less, and any given bond was becoming more risky (Temin 1976, pp. 107–108). The largest firms had access to credit at costs far lower than smaller firms. The cross-sectional pattern of industrial decline shows, however, that access to credit did not determine which industries declined.

At about the same time as the stock-market crash, the prices of raw materials and agricultural goods—which had

already been tending slowly downward—began to fall precipitously. Kindleberger identified the fall in commodity prices as one of the primary channels through which deflation spread, from "stock prices to commodity prices to the reduced value of imports." Although a change in prices only reallocates income, he argued, the effect is asymmetric. The losers found their budgets curtailed and were forced to cut spending; the winners did not correspondingly increase theirs (Kindleberger 1986, pp. 112–114, 136).

The prices of agricultural products and raw materials had been falling in the 1920s as a result of the overexpansion of production during and after the First World War. Various attempts to prop them up through tariffs or purchases had proved ineffective. Stocks accumulated as the production of many raw materials exceeded demand at the market price. The costs of holding these stocks and conducting orderly marketing rose as credit conditions were tightened at the end of the 1920s. In the credit squeeze that always came to the United States in the fall, many owners of these stocks failed in 1929. Further price declines were of course in store as the demand for raw materials contracted (Lewis 1949, p. 46; Svennilson 1954, ch. 5).

The effects of the price declines on different groups needs to be distinguished. For countries whose agricultural or mineral products were the main source of foreign currency, the fall in price was a disaster. Devaluations were the frequent response. But for importing countries, the decline in product prices was a plus. Even if Kindleberger is right and the price decline did not cause spending to rise, it allowed greater monetary ease. The United States experienced both effects. Farmers suffered, while the rest of the economy gained. The net effect of the initial fall in commodity prices in the United States therefore probably

was positive, since there were many more consumers than producers of these commodities in the United States.

The gain was limited, however, as prices in general began to decline in 1930. The more pervasive deflation cannot be attributed to the breakdown of cartels, and it was not closely correlated with the stock market. It was a reflection of the falling aggregate demand that came from the preceding credit stringency. Both the stock-market crash and the collapse of raw material prices were part of the propagating mechanism by which this tightness affected economic activity, but they were only part of a complex picture.

There are two effects of a general deflation, static and dynamic. The static effect, known sometimes as the Keynes effect, is to increase monetary ease. A given nominal stock of money buys more goods; real balances rise. In terms of the model of lecture 1, the aggregate supply curve is steep.[10] The fall in aggregate demand affects prices more than production. The deflation *substitutes* for depression.

The dynamic effect, known sometimes as the Mundell effect, works through expectations. If people expect the deflation to continue, they anticipate that prices will be even lower in the future than they are now. They hold off on purchases to take advantage of the expected lower prices. They are reluctant to borrow at any nominal interest rate because they will have to pay back the loan in dollars that are worth more when prices are lower than they are now. In short, the real interest rate rises above the nominal rate. The deflation *causes* depression (Tobin 1975; De Long and Summers 1986).

This can be incorporated into an IS-LM model by recognizing that the interest rate in the IS curve is the real rate, but that the interest rate in the LM curve is the nominal rate. No distinction needs to be made in a static model, like

the model of lecture 1. In the equilibrium which is the focus of models like that one, prices are constant, and the real and nominal interest rates are the same. A second, dynamic model therefore underlies the analysis in this lecture. In addition to making explicit the difference between the real and nominal interest rates, the model needs to allow a shock to have persistent effects and inflation or deflation to develop. Taylor's (1979) model of staggered wage contracts provides a convenient way for shocks to have effects in more than one period, allowing inflationary or deflationary expectations to flower. The result is a model in which flexible prices destabilize an economy. The details are shown in appendix A.

This model was presented by De Long and Summers (1986) as a conceptual device. They assumed rational expectations in their simulations, without inquiring into the actual path of expectations in any historical period. Application of this model to the Depression therefore requires a specification of expectations consistent with the historical evidence of 1929 and 1930. I have argued from a reading of the business press that this dynamic effect was not important in the opening stages of the Depression in the United States (Temin 1976). Leaving to later the question of what happened in late 1931 and 1932, I maintained that the deflation of 1930 was not expected to continue. This conclusion must be tempered slightly. The business community and investors were aware of the policy stance taken by the Federal Reserve and the government. They consequently must have had some fear that the deflationary policies would work and that prices would indeed fall. The revaluation of stocks that we call the stock-market crash was in part a reflection of that fear.

Recent work has tended to confirm the view that expectations of deflation were not widespread in 1930. Dominguez, Fair, and Shapiro (1988) examined the fore-

casts of the Harvard Economic Service and Irving Fisher at Yale. Although these observers were slightly outside the business community, they were making widely touted macroeconomic forecasts. They were considered knowledgeable about the workings of the economy and able to see through the maze of current information into underlying trends. Both of these groups maintained their belief in a rapid recovery through 1930. They acknowledged the obvious decline of business that had already taken place, but they did not anticipate its continuation.

In other words, these forecasters observed the changes taking place around them. These changes in economic variables, however, did not move them to alter their *expectations* about what was to come. The Harvard service argued that the current decline was like the short depression of 1920–21; Fisher asserted it was even milder. Only late in 1931, after the European financial crisis and the start of what I have called the second phase of the Depression, did their expectations become bearish.

Dominguez, Fair, and Shapiro also asked whether a modern observer, armed with the statistical tools of the later 1980s, could have done better with the time series used by the forecasters. In addition to giving the forecasters the benefit of modern technique, they added a few data series that have been compiled retrospectively to their inquiry. The results were quite striking. The revised forecasts fared no better than the historical ones. Even with modern tools and expanded data sources, the time-series data in 1929 and 1930 did not suggest that the good times had ended. Forecasts from 1929 did not indicate a downturn; forecasts from 1930 indicated a speedy recovery.

One exception to the pervasive optimism implicit in the time-series data is worth noting. Dominguez, Fair, and Shapiro made some forecasts using modern data from 1907 to 1930 to show how they differed from forecasts using

data available at the time and for shorter duration. These forecasts were still bullish on production. The difference was in the price forecasts. This group of forecasts predicted in 1929 that there would be a severe deflation, sometimes even faster than the actual one. But even in these cases information that came available in 1930 suggested that the deflation was over. Forecasts starting in the middle or at the end of 1930 did not predict continued deflation. These forecasts confirm the widespread view that the deflation had run its course.

American forecasters reasoned that the contraction would be brief on two independent grounds: the parallel with 1921 and time-series data for the whole decade of the 1920s. European observers reacted similarly. The German government, for example, did not anticipate continued depression until 1931 (Borchardt 1979, 1984).[11]

Since the depression of 1920–21 was a model for expectations in 1929–30, it is worth a slight detour to examine the earlier incident. Kindleberger argued that the dynamic effect of deflation was powerful in the first phase of the Depression, implicitly opposing the evidence just presented about expectations. He then had to ask why the Depression had not taken place in 1921, given the rapid deflation at that time. Unable to answer his question, he remarked that "the task of distinguishing between the episodes analytically remains unfinished" (Kindleberger 1986, pp. 136–141). I disagree with his premise that the deflation caused the Depression, but I still want to take up the challenge of distinguishing between the episodes.

The parallels are clear. Real GNP fell by 10 percent in both 1920–21 and 1929–30. Wholesale prices also fell in both years, by 10 percent in 1930 and by one-third in 1921. Prices had been rising in 1920 but not in 1929. The net price movement over two years therefore was more similar—a fall of about one-quarter—than over one year (U.S. Bureau

of the Census 1975, pp. 199, 234). The coincidence ends there, for recovery came rapidly in 1921 but only briefly and abortively in 1930. Why the difference?

The two depressions developed along different lines because they were fundamentally different in origin. Macroeconomic models (including those in appendix A) typically only talk about a single commodity. This clearly is an abstraction; the economy produces many goods. It follows that lower production may be the result of not only the traditional culprit, lack of aggregate demand, but also of shifts in the composition of demand. If demand shifts between industries, those losing demand will lay off workers. Industries with increasing demand will attempt to hire workers, but it takes time to reallocate workers. Unemployment is the result (Lilien 1982).[12]

The decline that started in 1929 was due to a failure of aggregate demand, as documented in lecture 1. The depression of 1920–21, by contrast, was due largely to a shift of demand. The war had ended, and demobilization resulted in a massive transfer of demand among industries and firms. In the United States, government expenditures contracted sharply in 1920, reducing demand and releasing workers. But the war had suppressed private demand and increased private wealth. The United States had borrowed from its citizens and loaned to allied governments, making a rapid transition from international borrower to international lender. As a result private demand rose to take the place of war expenditures. This wealth effect made for a short depression after the war. The comparable effect was strong enough to obviate any recession after the Second World War.

The federal debt rose by a factor of ten in the four years of World War I, as opposed to a factor of seven in the seven years following 1939. It was, however, only 30 percent of GNP at its peak in 1919, as opposed to 130 percent in 1946.

The effect of the increase in wealth from this source therefore was smaller after the First World War than after the Second, although still present (U.S. Bureau of the Census 1975, pp. 224, 1117). The United States also had new foreign assets after the war. It went from being a net debtor of at least $3.5 billion in 1914 to a net creditor of over $7 billion three years later (Studenski and Kroos 1963, pp. 280–284). Although there is some double counting in these measures, it is clear that there was the basis for an expansion of postwar aggregate demand.

Returning to the contrast between 1920 and 1929, conditions in Europe also were very different. In particular, Germany was in the midst of an inflation in the earlier year. The chronic inability of the Weimar government to contain the demands of diverse social groups and balance its budget was making its appearance in the years just after the war. Since the total reparations bill had not been set, it appeared to the Germans that restraint would benefit only foreigners, not themselves. Inflation and expansion was the result. German national income rose sharply in 1921, in contrast to its 1929 fall (Holtfrerich 1986, ch. 7). (The rise in national income was 8 percent in 1913 prices and 20 percent in 1928 prices.)

Therefore despite the similar speed of contraction at the beginning and end of the 1920s, the fall in aggregate demand was much larger in 1929. No actions were taken to counteract the fall. The parallel with 1921 implied that none was necessary. The theory of the gold standard indicated that expansion would be harmful. Neither the fiscal nor monetary authorities moved to restore aggregate demand. The deflationary shock that caused the downturn was allowed to spread through the economy unchecked.

As Friedman and Schwartz have repeatedly emphasized, the Federal Reserve was not constrained to stand by while the economic crisis intensified. Even if the Fed had

not wanted to intervene to help banks or depositors, they could have engaged in open market purchases that would have offset in whole or in part the existing deflationary pressures. They did not do so. They inferred from the low level of borrowed bank reserves in the early 1930s that monetary conditions were loose and that no action was needed. This was a poor indicator. It is total reserves that matter; the demand for borrowed reserves in the 1920s was largely to offset undesired movements in unborrowed reserves. And the fall in the borrowed reserves in 1930 and 1931 reflected the decline in the demand for money and therefore for total reserves. It was a sign of the Depression, not of monetary ease in a healthy economy (Wheelock 1988).

The German monetary and fiscal authorities topped this poor performance—they added to the decline in aggregate demand. The effects of credit restrictions in Germany were pervasive. The credit scarcity began to affect production in 1928. The German Railway Company was forced to abandon its ambitious six-year investment plan after only about a year at the start of 1928. Municipalities continued to borrow at higher interest rates, but many—including Berlin—faced bankruptcy by 1929. Public utilities, housing, manufacturing, all experienced difficulties (Balderston 1983). The German credit markets were tight even though the money supply was rising. The German money supply only began to contract in July 1930, and falling prices turned this decline into a continued rise in real balances (James 1984).

Heinrich Brüning became Germany's chancellor in March 1930. He governed with decreasing parliamentary support, particularly after the dramatic Nazi gains in the September 1930 election. His cabinet was increasingly composed of apolitical experts, men loyal to the dictates of traditional public finance rather than to current needs. Their deflationary impulses were strengthened by the

German government's inability to finance a deficit. The Reichsbank in particular was unwilling to initiate a policy of fiscal and financial expansion even slightly reminiscent of the hyperinflation (Balderston 1982). Brüning therefore issued a series of austerity decrees, increasing taxes, reducing government benefits and wages, and—in the second phase of the Depression—cutting prices, wages, and interest rates (James 1986, pp. 32–34).

The German monetary and fiscal authorities were victims of their history, and it is hardly surprising that they acted as they did. But it is not quite accurate to say they were constrained by their history. Conditions in 1930 did not reproduce those of 1922 and 1923, despite the continuing strains in German society and its economy. The economic distance between the Brüning deflation and hyperinflation was huge; it would have allowed room for expansion to leaders less fettered by gold-standard ideas.

Government expenditures in Britain rose in 1930, as did the component of public spending directed toward goods and services. The increase in the latter, however, was only about 5 percent in real terms—which was about 0.5 percent of GNP. Although mildly expansionary, British fiscal policy could not keep unemployment from rising from 10 to 16 percent. A more active stance was blocked by the prevailing orthodoxy (parallel to the views we have seen in the United States) which dictated that greater expenditures and government deficits would destroy confidence and crowd out private activity (Winch 1969). As stated in a memorandum to Ramsey Macdonald in July 1930, the government had to "sweep away ruthlessly any lingering illusions that a substantial reduction of unemployment figures [was] to be sought in the artificial provision of employment" (Aldcroft 1970, pp. 302–316).

The hearings of the Macmillan committee (also in 1930) gave Keynes ample opportunity to press his opposing

views. But mustered against the weight of economic orthodoxy, he could only—as Macmillan characterized one
memorable debate—fight his opponents to a draw. He,
along with everyone else, was debating within the confines of the gold standard. For Keynes, surely, this was
fighting with one hand tied behind his back (Harrod 1951,
pp. 413–431).

During the first phase of the Depression, the static
Keynes effect dominated. As the second phase ap-
proached, the dynamic Mundell effect rose to the fore.
Self-fulfilling expectations of further decline grew in
strength. It is impossible to date the change with any preci-
sion because we do not have sensitive indicators of expectations. But it is clear that the change to deflationary
expectations had been made by the spring of 1931. Expectations were catching up to events. Having experienced
a year or more of rapid deflation, people began to expect
more and to delay expenditures until the deflation ended
(Lewis 1949, p. 56). As Fisher (1933) pointed out only a few
years later, the deflation also increased the real value of
debts, leading to a reduction in spending independent of
changing expectations. Doubts about the stability of the re-
constructed gold-standard regime encouraged destabilizing speculation (Hamilton 1988). The tenuous gold standard of the interwar period was deflationary in a way that
the more solid Victorian gold standard had not been.

The string of banking panics and currency crises of that
summer and fall gives eloquent testimony to the pervasiveness of deflationary anticipations. In terms of the De Long
and Summers model, the Mundell effect dominated. The
expected real interest rate rose above the nominal rate. Private observers—as opposed to dogmatic public figures—
were no longer taken in by the apparent parallel with the
short depression of 1921, and they exhibited at least partial
understanding of the events they were witnessing. In this

second stage of the Depression, price declines had turned from being expansionary to being contractionary.

The second phase was ushered in by the failure of the Credit Anstalt, Austria's largest bank. The Credit Anstalt had unwisely operated during the 1920s as if the Hapsburg empire had not been broken up. An auditor's report in May 1931 revealed the parlous position of the bank, setting off a run on the bank that spread to the Austrian schilling. The government quickly ran through its foreign exchange reserves in a vain attempt to adhere to the gold standard and only belatedly imposed foreign-exchange controls (Stiefel 1989).

The German banking crisis of July 1931 often is seen as the consequence of the Austrian financial collapse in May. But the German banks survived the Austrian crash, and the problems oppressing the Brüning government were temporarily alleviated in June. The threat of a vote of no confidence in the Reichstag diminished with an agreement on June 15, and Hoover's moratorium on political debts was announced five days later.

Yet the pressure on German banks intensified. Table 2.2 shows some of the relevant data. James (1984) reported the bank reserves in cash and deposits at the Reichsbank. He showed that the banks kept reserves of under 3 percent of deposits, often less than 2 percent, from 1928 to 1934. At the time of the banking crisis in mid-1931, however, these reserves were increasing, not decreasing, as was the reserve ratio of banks.

No grounds for a banking panic consequently appear in James' data. This creates the suspicion that he was not looking at the appropriate magnitudes. In fact reserves of this miniscule size do not seem like reserves at all. They probably were vault cash, that is, cash on hand to meet emergency needs, to be supplemented by the rest of reserves in a matter of days.

**Table 2.2**
German banking data, 1931
(end of month)

| Month | Deposits | Reserves (RM million) | | Reserve ratios (percent) | |
|-------|----------|-------|------------|-------|------------|
|       |          | James | Balderston | James | Balderston |
| January |  |  |  |  |  |
| February | 18385 | 274 | 6475 | 1 | 35 |
| March | 18317 | 404 | 6506 | 2 | 36 |
| April | 18281 | 310 | 6612 | 2 | 36 |
| May | 17747 | 363 | 6315 | 2 | 36 |
| June | 16061 | 389 | 4923 | 2 | 31 |
| July | 15064 | 484 | 3997 | 3 | 27 |
| August | 14333 | 274 | 4041 | 2 | 28 |
| September | 13884 | 368 | 3896 | 3 | 28 |
| October | 13384 | 288 | 3664 | 2 | 27 |
| November | 13260 | 268 | 3713 | 2 | 28 |
| December |  |  |  |  |  |

Sources: James (1984); Balderston (1988).

Data from the United States provide comparison. Vault cash in the United States also was about 2 percent of bank deposits in mid-1931. But bank reserves were composed of vault cash plus deposits at Federal Reserve banks. Vault cash was only one-quarter of total bank reserves. Although vault cash shows how prepared banks are for the moment, it is reserves that matter for the fate of banks over more than a few days. Attention in America rightly has been directed toward bank reserves, not their vault cash. (Before the Fed was created, vault cash and bank reserves were identical. But vault cash then was far greater than 2 percent of deposits. Banks held enough vault cash to bring their reserves up to the range of 10 to 15 percent of deposits

before World War I. See Friedman and Schwartz 1963, app. A.)

There was no Federal Reserve in Germany, but there was the Reichsbank. Although banks had deposits at the Reichsbank, they were small and did not play the role of deposits at the Federal Reserve in the United States. Instead, banks held the bulk of their reserves in checks, bills of exchange, and Treasury bills that could be freely discounted at the Reichsbank. They undoubtedly earned more than deposits at the Reichsbank and were equally liquid as long as the Reichsbank stood ready to purchase them. (I am indebted to T. Balderston, University of Manchester, for this information. See Germany 1934.)

The parallel with the United States is not exact. The Reichsbank was not the Federal Reserve. Banks in the United States had the legal right to convert reserves into cash if needed. German banks had to rely on the Reichsbank to purchase their bills. This meant that the reserves of the German banks were not as secure as those of their American counterparts. It also meant that the Reichsbank had less control over the money supply. Despite the imperfect analogy, the total reserves were a more important determinant of bank behavior than the vault cash component.

Reserves calculated on this basis are shown in table 2.2, under Balderston, as is the recalculated reserve ratio. The reserve ratio of banks fell sharply in June 1931, and again in July. This was the sign of the mounting crisis. Reserves fell by 1.4 billion Reichsmarks in June and an additional 0.9 billion in July. Of this total, fully two-thirds in each month was accounted for by a reduction in the amount of bills held by banks. This reduction was concentrated almost entirely in the six great Berlin banks, and it was paralleled by a rise in the Reichsbank portfolio of virtually the exact same size. The large Berlin banks were selling their bills to

the Reichsbank. They sold over half of their bill portfolio in those two months (Balderston 1988).

The German banks were not running out of vault cash; they were running out of reserves. Depositors were cashing in their deposits for cash; deposits at the large Berlin banks fell by the same amount as their reserves in these months. The banks then were replenishing their cash from the Reichsbank. The failure of the Nordwolle put special pressure on the DANAT Bank, whose reserves fell by two-thirds between May and August. The deposit withdrawals represented capital flight by Germans, joined by Americans only at the tail end of the process (Bennett 1962; James 1984; Balderston 1988).

The problem was not even primarily that the banks were losing reserves, except for the DANAT Bank. It was that the Reichsbank lacked the assets to monetize the banks' reserves (James 1985). Despite credits from other central banks, the Reichsbank had fallen below its statutory requirement of 40 percent reserves by the beginning of July, and it was unable to borrow more from the other central banks. The French, who had the reserves to lend, were still fighting the First World War. They tied political strings around their offer of help that had the unwitting effect of prolonging the Second Thirty Years' War (Einzig 1932). They were not alone in aggravating an already bad situation. The Germans tried their best to use the crisis to renegotiate the peace settlement and eliminate reparations, while the Americans pulled in the opposite direction to isolate the German banking crisis from any long-run considerations (Bennett 1962).

The Reichsbank raised interest rates in late June. But Reichsbank President Hans Luther did not follow Bagehot's (1873) advice in this circumstance: raise interest rates, but lend freely. The Reichsbank refused to discount bills of firms thrown into difficulty by the tightened credit. The

result was to further dampen domestic industry without markedly reducing the panic (Clarke 1967; James 1984).

James argued that the German banking crisis was best understood as an example of Minsky's "financial-instability hypothesis" in which changes over a boom "transform an initially robust financial system into a fragile financial system" (Minsky 1982, p. 24). This portrays the German crisis as an inevitable result of the five prosperous years following 1924. I think this is a misinterpretation. The German banking crisis of 1931 showed instead how three years of deflation can destabilize a financial system. It showed one dramatic way in which changing expectations came to destabilize the world economy. As people came to expect the deflation to continue, they tried to protect themselves as best they could from business and financial failures, causing further contraction—at least in Germany. The German currency crisis was part of the deflation necessitated by adherence to the rules of the gold-standard game.

A series of presidential decrees in the week following July 15, 1931, imposed controls over German foreign exchange transactions. Permission was required for all foreign exchange transactions. They had to go through the Reichsbank or its agents and be at the official rate. The import and export of currency and gold by individuals was banned. Standstill agreements were negotiated with the governments of Germany's creditors in August, providing that short-term credits to Germany would be drawn down slowly or, in the case of trade credits, not at all. These controls were designed to arrest the capital flight of the moment. They were a temporary expedient, allowing the speedy resumption of normal international commerce (Child 1958, pp. 15–22).

The controls, of course, were anything but temporary. But unfortunately they did not signal a change in the government's deflationary policy. Brüning's and Luther's aim was to surmount the problems of the moment; they were undeviating in their belief that deflation was needed to solve the underlying imbalance. The imposition of exchange controls freed Germany from some of the excess of the gold standard. It did not free it from the grip of gold-standard ideology. Brüning's most draconian decree was issued in December 1931. The Reichsbank lowered interest rates from their punitive levels at the height of the currency crisis, but this was part of the price reductions, not a sign of easy money. Access to credit at the published rate was restricted (Ellis 1941, p. 176; Child 1958, p. 28).

Was this policy unavoidable? Borchardt has argued forcefully in a series of recent articles that it was, that the problems of the German economy did not provide the basis for an alternative path. In his 1979 article he argued that the need for expansionary policy was not apparent until the summer of 1931. Then both monetary and fiscal expansion were precluded by political, legal, and economic barriers. Borchardt did not discuss devaluation at that time. He extended his argument to include devaluation in a subsequent paper, arguing that there was no political constituency for such a move (Borchardt 1979, 1980, 1984).

Borchardt argued within the framework of the gold standard. He provided reasons why certain actions could not have been undertaken within that framework. A better question is whether Brüning could have—by stepping outside this ideological straitjacket—set the German economy on a different course. This is a much disputed question, but I think that abandoning the gold standard by devaluation could well have relieved much of the deflationary pressure on Germany.

Had the Reichsmark been allowed to float, it would have fallen to a point where further capital flight was no longer desirable. There would have been some gyrations along the way, magnified by the prevalent fears of another hyperinflation. The British example of a few months later suggests, however, that the instability would not have been marked, even though the British had not had the recent history of instability of the Germans. Exchange controls similar to those instituted in the summer of 1931 would have avoided many of the ill effects of speculation. Freed of the need to maintain gold exports, domestic expansion ruled out by the factors Borchardt cited would have become possible. The American experience in 1933 shows how a crisis like the German one could have been managed to effect an orderly devaluation.

But devaluation was not a popular policy in Germany. There was, as Borchardt has detailed, no political constituency for it. This can hardly be an argument against devaluation. Brüning's deflationary policy also lacked a political constituency. He did not have support in the Reichstag, he lost support in repeated elections, and he had to people his cabinet with apolitical experts. It is hard to argue that his political fortunes would have been harmed by devaluation.

Other arguments given against a German devaluation are of some interest. There are at least five in the literature. Devaluation would increase capital flight. It would increase the value of Germany's foreign debt. It would be negated by wage inflation. It was associated with the inflation of 1923, and it was illegal (Child 1958, p. 27; Overy 1982, pp. 21–23; Borchardt 1984).

None of these reasons is compelling. The argument that devaluation would increase capital flight confuses the cure with the disease. Capital was fleeing because people holding Reichsmarks were afraid the currency would lose its value. Once devaluation had taken place, only the expectation of further devaluation would have led to flight. In any case further flight would only lower the price of the mark,

leading other people to want to buy it. Devaluation therefore would have reduced capital flight and its effects, not
increased it.

Germany's war debts were suspended for one year by
the Hoover moratorium and then canceled a year later at
Lausanne. The large private debts remained. But the extra
depreciated marks that would have had to be paid to service them are small relative to the value of foregone output. The foreign debt was all new; the previous debt had
been wiped out by the hyperinflation. The debt service in
1931 consequently was about 10 percent of German exports
(Schuker 1988, p. 65). Increases in this ratio from devaluation would not be negligible, but they were hardly the
worst thing that could overtake the German economy.

Wage inflation could well have offset a large part of any
devaluation. Even so, there would be benefits to the economy. The government would have been freed to undertake more expansionary policies. Social discontent would
have been eased, relaxing the political pressure on the
Brüning (or successor) government. As people acknowledged the end of the deflation, the real interest rate would
have dropped. Private industry would have been encouraged to invest. Even if competitive devaluation reduced
the relative price effects, more expansionary expectations
would have encouraged the resumption of production (see
appendix A).

The risk is that these expansionary impulses could not
have been controlled. Public expenditures would rise
again. The inflation would rise out of control. Production
would be distorted and interrupted as it had been in the
1923 inflation. The mark would collapse.

Historians can differ on the likelihood of this prospect. It
clearly depends on expectations that are hard to recon-
struct. The memory of the hyperinflation was only part of
the problem. The German government was bound to pre-

serve the value of the mark in its laws and in the Dawes and Young Plans. Would abrogation of that rule have been seen as the proper response to an emergency or as one more example of German unwillingness to accept the judgment of the war? Might the French have responded as strongly as they did in 1923 and invade?

There is a long way from the four million unemployed of mid-1931 to a hyperinflation, and it is unlikely that it would have been taken without determined expansion by the German government. But even a certain amount of chaos on the way to recovery might well have been preferable to the historical alternative: the rise of Hitler. The Depression in Germany led to the most terrible results. It is hard to argue that any alternative would have been worse.

This is an admittedly ahistorical view. It nevertheless contains an important point. One test of an alternative policy in 1931 is whether it would have functioned well according to some absolute standard. Another is whether the outcome would have been preferable to the historical actuality. The latter test is typically in our minds even if we profess to follow the former. It is worth confronting it directly. No one in 1931 could have been expected to have foreseen the horrors of the Nazi era, but the Nazi gains in the 1930 election showed clearly the growing disintegration of Weimar society. We should hope that leaders in future crises will take into account the possibility of totalitarian takeover when they make their economic choices.

Despite this retrospective logic, the pressure on the Reichsmark was contained by exchange controls, not devaluation. The international panic spread to the pound. The Bank of England was unwilling to raise Bank Rate, which it kept relatively low throughout the crisis. It then had to support the pound by direct intervention, that is, by buying pounds from whoever wanted to sell. It needed reserves to make these purchases, which it lacked. Credits from the United States and France were negotiated in July and spent in August. New credits were obtained in August, which went the way of the old. On September 20, 1931, the Bank of England threw in the towel and announced the suspension of the gold standard (Cairncross and Eichengreen 1983; Kunz 1987).

Montagu Norman fled England in July, foreshadowing the British flight from gold two months later. He was absent during the critical weeks of decision but probably was consulted and had concurred. Norman's aim, and the aim of the British authorities more generally, was to appear as the victims of circumstance, not as initiators of action (Kunz 1987).

The British devaluation is almost universally viewed as a policy failure, partly in response to the way in which it was done. But in my view it was a (limited) policy success. Keynes recommended devaluation at the beginning of August, before (as he said) converting sterling obligations into franc and dollar liabilities (Howson and Winch 1977, p. 89). The British trade balance improved markedly as the depreciation of the pound encouraged exports and discouraged imports. This provided a stimulus to domestic production that arrested the contraction. The monetary and fiscal authorities were freed to adopt more expansionary policies. The policy was of only limited success, however, because the British authorities did not take advantage of this opportunity as they should have. Instead, they raised Bank Rate to replenish their depleted reserves and to fight inflation, in other words, "to cry, Fire, Fire, in Noah's Flood," as Hawtrey phrased it (Hawtrey 1938, p. 145; Cairncross and Eichengreen 1983, pp. 83–103).

The British economy did not recover in 1932. As shown in figure 1.1, British production stagnated. Though not lifting Britain out of the Depression, devaluation lifted it out of the contraction. The Depression was not shorter, but it was milder than in other countries. This was due in part to the continuation of deflationary policies in Britain, even after the need for them was gone. Both Germany and Britain fought an inflation that did not exist (Robbins 1934, pp. 112–114; Kindleberger 1986, pp. 158–164).

Britain's achievement, though perhaps not spectacular, is still deserving of notice. The condemnation of Britain's devaluation has blinded historians. James (1986, p. 284), for example, said that, "In states where there was no great threat of banking collapse, such as Britain, the interwar depression was much milder [than in Germany]." This statement confuses correlation with causation. The British devaluation was instrumental in encouraging both domestic financial health and a partial recovery; they were the joint result of the devaluation.

Kindleberger (1986, pp. 158–162, 187) argued that Britain's devaluation was bad for the rest of the world, whether it helped Britain itself or not. He asserted in particular that the fall in the value of the pound decreased world prices of raw materials, citing data on the price of a variety of commodities in support. The data, however, do not support this view. Prices fell *before* Britain went off gold. They did not fall faster afterward. Figure 2.3 shows wholesale commodity prices and the price of pounds, both in dollars, for 1930 to 1936. It is clear that commodity prices fell before the change in the exchange rate. There was no discernible break in the rate of decline of monthly prices when Britain left gold. (Prices did rise when the United States left gold—but that is part of lecture 3.)

Britain's devaluation therefore was not a powerful contractionary impulse. As a result of the Bank of England's concern to rebuild its gold reserves, Britain did not release gold to the rest of the world, promoting worldwide expansion. The devaluation therefore must be counted as a beggar-thy-neighbor policy (see appendix A for details).

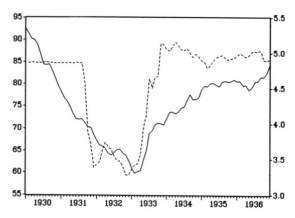

**Figure 2.3**
Wholesale commodity prices and the exchange rate, 1930–1936.
*Solid line*: wholesale commodity prices in dollars (1926 = 100);
*dotted line*: value of the pound in dollars. Source: Commodity
Research Bureau (1939, p. 495); Federal Reserve System (1943, p.
681).

And it set off speculation, directed this time toward the
dollar, which I will discuss shortly. These negative effects
were offset by the possibility of British expansion and by
the example Britain gave to other countries. Unhappily,
this message was clouded by the orthodox interpretation
of the devaluation, which viewed it as a policy failure.
True, it was done under duress; but it was still the right
thing to do.

In the view I have taken here, it was an ironic achievement. If the gold standard was the downfall of the interwar
economy, then surely Britain was the villain. The gold
standard had been the vehicle through which British
prosperity was spread in the late nineteenth century to re-
bound back on the home country. Its restoration after the
war was championed by Britain in all kinds of forums.
Although the British were hardly alone in this endeavor, as

I tried to show in lecture 1, they were the primary proponents. Yet, while other countries allowed their economies to go to pieces under the strain of staying on gold, the British opted out. They were the first major country to leave gold. It was the world's tragedy that other countries did not follow its lead.

The German government contemplated devaluation briefly after the British left gold (James 1985, pp. 287–291; Schuker 1988, p. 62). Much of the sting had gone out of this action by then. It is unlikely that the Germans would have been punished for violating this requirement of the Young Plan after the British had walked away from their obligations under the gold standard. Germany had instituted currency controls that would have contained any destabilizing speculation. Fears of a collapse of the mark should have been laid to rest by the relatively calm British experience. Brüning had the perfect opportunity to jump off the gold-standard train. Even if a German devaluation had been fraught with unknowable difficulties in July, it would have been a reasonable policy in October—far, far better than Brüning's deflationary decree of December.

The French were not tempted to follow Britain, given their large gold holdings. They did not seem to be aware that their undervalued franc was becoming an overvalued franc as the Depression deepened. The French money supply, which had been rising through 1930, began a decline that would last for five years (Patat and Lutfalla 1987).

Conditions in the United States were promising for an act similar to Britain's. What Friedman and Schwartz called the first banking panic was an isolated set of failures in late 1930. The rate of bank failures, as shown in figure 2.2, returned to its prior level for the first four months of 1931. Friedman and Schwartz dated the second banking panic from March 1931. But it can be seen from the graph that bank failures actually were low in March 1931. They rose in

May, fell back to their previous level in June, and then rose for several months starting in July. Friedman and Schwartz's dating makes banking difficulties in the United States appear to have been quite separate from those in Europe. In fact bank failures were high in the United States in the summer of 1931, which was the same time as the European currency crises.

The Federal Reserve, of course, opted to preserve the value of the dollar. It raised interest rates and—again violating Bagehot's dictum—accelerated the decline in the money supply. The result was that interest rates in the United States rose sharply in the fourth quarter of 1931, and credit became harder to get. Industrial production—which had paused briefly in its descent in the spring of 1931—continued to contract. The Depression in the United States intensified.

Unlike the "first banking crisis," the Fed's response to Britain's devaluation is clearly visible in the growth of the money supply. Figure 2.4 shows the rate of growth of the money stock bouncing around in the eighteen months prior to the British devaluation with a slight downward trend. The rate of growth was at or below the low point of its previous rates in August and September 1931. It fell to the lowest rate of growth in this three-year period in October, just after the British devaluation. In addition the money supply declined more rapidly in the following months than it had in the previous two years (see appendix B for a more formal treatment).

The Fed's open market purchases of 1932 were in part a response to the clamor for expansion in response to the monetary contraction of late 1931. They succeeded only in restoring the rate of money growth to the low levels prevailing before the summer of 1931 (figure 2.4). They were abandoned by midyear for a variety of reasons. Banks had increased the proportion of Treasury bills in their port-

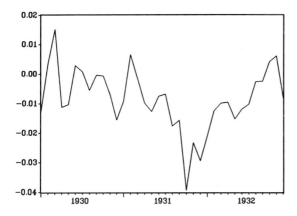

**Figure 2.4**
Growth of the money stock, 1930–32 (first difference of the logarithm of M2). Source: Friedman and Schwartz (1963, table A1).

folios as loans became harder to place. Therefore, to the extent that interest rates fell, they reduced earnings of banks holding bills and threatened their already precarious solvency. The Fed's objectives as overseer of the nation's banks and of the national economy come into conflict. In addition some Federal Reserve banks were running out of "free gold," that is, excess reserves on their currency. The Federal Reserve banks were unwilling to pool their reserves by interbank borrowing, and the effective reserve of the system was set by the weakest banks. Finally, the French and then the British began to withdraw their dollar balances in New York (Epstein and Ferguson 1984).

The British position in this episode was not expansionary. Having gone off gold, the Bank of England was free to pursue a cheap money policy. But it was worried about an appreciation of sterling caused by low American interest rates that diverted short-term capital from the U.S. to Britain. Instead of countering by lowering its rates even more—an expansionary move for Britain—the Bank sold dollars—to exert a contractionary force on the United States.[13] The sale of dollars put pressure on the Fed to stop its open market purchases and reduce its expansionary impact. The British, despite the floating pound, were not willing to reach an equilibrium by expanding the economy. They still believed that international balance could only be achieved by contraction at home or abroad. It was not enough to go off gold; the gold-standard mentality had to be excised, the gold-standard policy regime abandoned.

The Federal Reserve was constrained in 1932, as it had been a year earlier, by the U.S. commitment to the gold standard. It was unwilling to sacrifice the gold value of the dollar to an economic expansion. The Fed's relations to its member banks were important; adherence to the gold standard is not the whole story. But it was a major theme of American behavior throughout the contraction, not simply in late 1931.

Britain moved also at this time to initiate steep import duties. It was too late in time to be considered retaliation for the Smoot-Hawley tariff, and trade with America was in any case a small part of Britain's foreign transactions. Enacted initially by the new National government in November 1931, the duties were transformed into Imperial Preference at Ottowa in the summer of 1932, even as the Fed's open market purchases were ending. France at the same time was replacing its tariffs with quotas, the tariffs having been rendered ineffectual by deflation and the British devaluation. Germany restricted trade through exchange controls that grew from a temporary expedient to a tool for managing trade (Friedman 1974).

Foreign trade dried up under the combined onslaught of Depression and trade restriction. Each country tried to maintain its own producers at the expense of foreigners. Individually the restrictions were beggar-thy-neighbor

policies. Is it fair to infer that they together had a deflationary impact? Might they—like devaluation—have been in-
nocent in the aggregate?

That is the conclusion of the Eichengreen and Sachs
model of lecture 1. Adding trade restrictions to the IS curve
(equation 8 in appendix A) provides a parallel with devaluation. Tariffs raise prices, with offsetting effects. The
price rise expands output through the aggregate supply
curve but reduces it through the fall in the real money
supply. If both countries restrict trade, the impulses mostly cancel out, leaving incomes largely unaffected. Demand
is reallocated between the (identical) countries, but the
total is more or less constant (Eichengreen 1989).

This result is in sharp contrast with the standard Keynesian model which shows a reduction in exports as a fall in
demand for each country (Lewis 1949). The difference derives, as always, from a difference of assumptions. The
Keynesian model assumes that resources used to produce
exports cannot be reallocated to domestic demand. The
model of lecture 1, by contrast, assumes that there is no
cost in such a redirection. Mutual trade restriction in this
model increases domestic demand at the same time as it
reduces export demand.

The actual experience was somewhere in the middle.
Demand choked off by quotas and tariffs did not simply
disappear; it was replaced by domestic demand. But the
transformation of assets was neither instantaneous nor
costless. Reallocated demand therefore was not a perfect
substitute for familiar patterns. Trade restrictions were
harmful, just not as bad as conventionally thought.

The historical outlines of this story are familiar. The link
between economics and politics has always been a major
factor, albeit not typically in the form revealed here. I have
argued that the virtually universal commitment to the gold
standard by political and economic leaders throughout the

major industrial countries determined the depth and severity of the Depression. This ideology generated what we now think of as perverse reactions to the deflationary that shocks being sent around the world. Although there were voices calling for expansion, the counsels of the powerful were dominated by deflationists.

The strength and pervasiveness of this ideology made it hard to break out of it. It made alternative policies difficult. They were not, however, impossible. To claim that they were inconceivable is to argue the inevitability of history. We regard those people as leaders who have been able to break out of the existing cast of thought and blaze new trails. That those in power were unable to do so shows that they were poor leaders, not that the task was impossible.

It is not as if deflation was wildly popular among the populace, so that any leader suggesting an alternative would be hounded out of office. Quite the reverse. The deflationists were on the political defensive. They clung to their conceptions despite public clamor to abandon them. They rejected proposals made by their opposition. They stayed the course.

They also lost elections. The German government lost seats in the Reichstag every time it called an election. The first signal came in September 1930, almost a year before the German currency crisis. Borchardt argued that no politician could have realized the need for expansionary policy before the currency crisis. The tremendous gains of the Nazis in the 1930 election, however, carried a frightening message if Brüning had wanted to see it. Historians have debated whether the German people wanted the Nazis only because of economic distress or because of other, darker factors as well (Hamilton 1982; Childers 1983). But it is clear that the vote of 1930 was a resounding rejection of Brüning's deflationary policy at an early stage.

Brüning's famous statement that he fell 100 meters from

the goal is doubly ironic (Stolper, Häuser, and Borchardt 1967, p. 121). It ignored the part that Brüning himself had played in the deepening Depression. The goal in this image stands apart from the players; it is not carried by the players as they move down the field. In addition the goal that Brüning saw was an end to Germany's reparations obligations. It was hardly a view of a prosperous economy or a stable polity. It was Germany's and the world's tragedy that Brüning had so little understanding of what he was doing and had done.

President Hoover also lost an election, although the timing of elections in America is fixed. He, like much of Brüning's cabinet, was a technocrat. He applied the principles of engineering to the economy and held to these principles even as the economy collapsed around him. His views evolved in the course of the Depression, but they became more conservative as the Depression intensified. He stayed within the confines of sound money and the gold standard. He was, as a result, resoundingly rejected by the Anerican people in the election of 1932.

An important element of this story is its international character. The major industrial countries were highly interdependent. Their actions affected each other in various ways. The origins of the Depression lay in the interaction of exchange rates and international capital movements. Its continuation lay in the transmission of currency crises and banking panics as well as in the diminution of commodity demands. It was hard for any single country to expand on its own, as shown by Britain in 1931 and the United States in 1932.

Even more important than the market interactions was the mutual support that the international financial community gave to the gold standard. A small group of bankers and ministers traveled around Europe and to America in the early 1930s, assuring each other of the vitality of their mission to save the gold standard. They recommended deflation, contraction, tightening up, in response to every problem. They confirmed each other's belief in the probity of their actions. They made it doubly hard for any single leader to break out of the mold.

Stories that deal only with one country, therefore, have trouble finding causes for the Depression commensurate with its severity. It is not hard to find a domestic explanation for the initial downturn. But it is hard to explain within a single country how this initial impulse was spread and intensified to produce three or four year of contraction. The propagation mechanism was international. A single-country story omits many links in the causal chain.

This view corresponds to those expressed by Kindleberger, even though I have disagreed with him on many specific points. It conflicts sharply with those of Friedman and Schwartz. They looked for an American cause of the Depression and were forced to pick a small event and argue for its worldwide impact. They searched for a propagation mechanism and found it in the American banking panics. The death of Strong was a minor aspect of a world deflation, as shown in lecture 1. The banking panics had little independent impact, as shown here.

In fact Friedman and Schwartz's dating of the banking crises does not hold up. They identified two banking crises before the European currency troubles in the summer of 1931. The first of these was an isolated movement related to the failure of two large banks that had little impact on the rate of change of the money supply and interest rates. The second of these was a slight rise in a period when the rate of failures had fallen back to its previous level. Neither of them was a major event.

The identification of these uniquely American "crises" was an important rhetorical device distinguishing America from Europe. It made the timing of American events a matter for domestic explanation, and it relegated European developments to the interstices of the argument.

Data on bank failures, however, show that the primary wave of failures in America came in the summer of 1931, at the same time when major European banks were in trouble. The coincidence of events is shown by the rate of change of the money supply, which fails to show the impact of the banking "crises." It does however, show clearly the effect of the Fed's reaction to the British devaluation, that is, to an international event. America was an important actor—perhaps the most important—in an ensemble production.

There are many morals to this play. Many of them concern the theory of rational expectations. More precisely, they stress the application of this theory. People, we know, can look at the same events and draw different conclusions. To model rational expectations therefore, we need to specify how people interpret the world around them. We need to specify the model that they are using.

This step is typically taken so fast that it is not noticed at all. The author assumes that the participants in the process he or she is describing use the same model as the author. The model can be closed and (usually) solved. Muth (1961, p. 316) himself included this assumption in his original definition. "I should like to suggest that expectations, since they are informed predictions of future events, are essentially the same as the predictions of the relevant economic theory."

The problem comes in the choice of the relevant economic theory. Even though people may make use of all the available information, they may interpret it with a flawed model. This is not "rational" in the usual sense. It nevertheless captures the essence of rational expectations if the range of experience of participants has not allowed them to find the true model.

This was precisely the case during the Great Depression. None of the policymakers, none of the investors, none of the consumers, had ever lived through a depression like this before. The annals of economic history did not contain a similar event. Contemporary actors therefore had to extrapolate out of the historical sample.

We use Keynesian models to analyze the Depression. That type of model was not available during the contraction. Although many elements of what we now call Keynesian analysis were under discussion in the early 1930s, the model was only formulated by Keynes as a result of the Depression. It took him half a decade to complete it and more time for people to understand it and reformulate it more cogently. It has been amended many times since then, and we use much modified versions today. It violates history to assume that people in the early 1930s were what we now call Keynesians.

They interpreted the evidence they had to the best of their ability—within their model of the economy. It was the model of financial orthodoxy, of the gold standard. It led central bankers, fiscal authorities, and political leaders to hold to policies we now regard as disastrous. But in their model it only looked like they had not stayed the course. Brüning looked back and remarked that he had fallen 100 meters from the goal. He had learned nothing; the evidence of the German contraction had not shaken his belief in economic orthodoxy.

Three lessons follow from this observation. First, we must be suspicious of models that assume economic actors think like economists. Rational expectations is a useful first step in modeling expectations, but it embodies assumptions that are very strong. Our theories are different from those in use during the Great Depression. There is no way that people living then could have thought along the lines we now use to model the economy. What is true of history is only slightly less true today. There cannot be any doubt that policymakers and most private leaders of finance and industry today have not had recent courses in macroeconomics. They cannot be expected to act in accordance with existing models. We must investigate models where people have different ways of interpreting the evidence.

Second, we must be wary of international cooperation. Every effort was made in 1931 to preserve the gold value of the mark, pound, and dollar. Britain has been roundly criticized, then and now, for losing that battle. But we would all have been better off if the leaders had thrown in the towel, either in the summer of 1931 or by following Britain's example in the fall. Cooperation to have a joint devaluation might have been good, but it was not an available alternative. The only kind of cooperation possible was under the gold-standard orthodoxy. More of this kind of cooperation would have been dysfunctional (Frankel and Rockett 1988). Cooperation, in other words, is not good in and of itself. Its usefulness depends on the purposes to which cooperation is bent.

Third, we should be suspicious of leaders who stay with policies whose intellectual underpinnings are gone. The fiscal policy of the Reagan administration was to produce balanced budgets according to the original theory of supply-side economics. That theory is no longer heard in polite circles, but the policies introduced under its mantle are still in force. The new Bush administration appears committed to the policies—"No new taxes!"—even if not to the theory. The Great Depression bears eloquent witness to the dangers of clinging to economic policies long after their utility has been replaced by growing danger.

In the final lecture, I will describe the benefits of adopting a new regime, however flawed.

# Socialism in Many Countries: The Recovery from the Great Depression

The preceding lectures have argued that unsuitable macro-economic policies caused the Depression. In particular, the policy of "sound finance" that was symbolized by adherence to the gold standard mandated deflation in circumstances where it was the worst of policies. The contraction was so long and deep because these policies were maintained long after it should have been obvious that they, and not the countries involved, were bankrupt.

There is a natural corollary to these views. The end of the economic decline should have come when these deflationary policies were abandoned. That is the first point to be made in this third lecture. The reversal of macroeconomic policy in the United States under Roosevelt and in Germany under Franz von Papen and then Hitler turned the economic tide in 1933.

This point raises two others in its wake. What replaced the abandoned policies? And, why did depressed conditions last throughout the 1930s in so many countries? I will propose answers to these questions in turn, once the turning point has been analyzed.

I will argue that the policies that replaced fiscal orthodoxy were expansionary and in large part socialist. These new policies were not always initiated by socialist parties. I will therefore use the term to refer to the policies' content more than their political associations. For example, the new policies combined what we would call macro- and microeconomic elements; policymakers believed in both expanding and managing the economy. The Depression ushered in an age of moderate socialism, albeit in many variations.

The new socialism was only partly successful in restoring prosperity for several reasons. The first and most important was that it was not always politically successful. Just as Brown (1956) first argued for Keynesianism, socialism could not work if it was not tried. The second reason was the diminution of the capital stock from three or four years of neglect; the lack of capital reduced employment opportunities. A third reason for continued unemployment was that national economic policies sometimes offset the capital scarcity by creating jobs and sometimes accentuated it by managing the economy in ways that perpetuated unemployment.

But I am getting ahead of the story. It is necessary to begin the analysis with the beginning of recovery. This raises a problem familiar to students of the Depression. There appear to have been two low points in industrial production, in 1932 and 1933, in both the United States and Germany (Federal Reserve System 1940; Henning 1973). Which one was the true nadir?

Statistical tests are no help. Looking only at the monthly indexes themselves, it is just as likely that the abortive recovery of 1932 was part of the way down as part of the way up. I want to argue, however, that the recovery started only in 1933. The earlier stirrings were not strong enough to turn the economic tide. The Federal Reserve's open market purchases of 1932 were halted after only a few months under pressure (as described in lecture 2), and the German employment programs under Brüning and Papen were small and tentative (as will be described below). Each impulse was strong enough to moderate the economic decline. Neither was strong enough to initiate recovery. As Irving Fisher (who was better at understanding than at predicting) observed at the time, "Those who imagine that Roosevelt's avowed reflation is not the cause of our recovery but that we had 'reached the bottom anyway' are very much mistaken" (Fisher 1933, p. 346).

In fact the Depression seemed to have the world by the throat in 1932. Business was bad everywhere. Hardly anyone expected to make money from new investments, and new investments consequently were few. Few jobs were secure, and many workers were getting used to unemployment as a way of life. The world seemed to be maladjusted with little hope of repair. There did not seem to be anything to do.

This, however, was wrong. The Depression only seemed to have a momentum of its own. The downward spiral was perpetuated and accelerated by the policy stance of governments and central banks in the major industrial countries. Contracts and investments had been made in the expectation of further deflation. But activities only reflected these expectations because government policies warranted these expectations.

Investors and workers were not responding to isolated government actions. They were acting in accord with what Sargent (1983) called the underlying policy regime. The regime is an abstraction from any single decision; it represents the systematic and predicable part of all decisions. It is the thread that runs though the individual choices that governments and central banks have to make. It is visible even though there inevitably will be some loose ends, that is, some decisions that do not fit the general pattern. These isolated actions have little impact because they represent exceptions to the policy rule, not new policy regimes.

It follows that it was not a trivial task to change the direction of the economy. People were locked into their bargains in the short run. More important, they had expectations about the policy regime that had to be changed. They regarded actions that departed from the deflationary policy regime initially as aberrations, individual actions that had no implications for the regime as a whole. They needed to be convinced that the regime had changed, not simply that the policy process was noisy.

There needed to be a dramatic and highly visible change in policy. There needed to be symbols of the change that could be widely understood and that — like good signals — had costs for policymakers adhering to the old regimes (Spence 1974). Sargent (1983) argued that a dramatic action would change expectations so quickly that the economy could reverse direction without bearing any cost of readjustment. Although Sargent's insight is very useful in understanding the beginning of recovery, there are several problems with his formulation. Garber (1982) and Wicker (1986) have shown that the currency stabilizations of the 1920s involved considerable costs. Changing expectations alone are not strong enough to turn an economy around. They need to be supplemented by effective macroeconomic policies. In addition Sargent concentrated on price expectations — as might be expected in an analysis of hyperinflations. Quantity movements were as important as price movements at the bottom of the Depression, and the analysis needs to treat expectations about the course of demand — whether they showed up in price or quantity movements. It is only Sargent's emphasis on changes in the policy regime that I wish to employ here.

I argued in lecture 2 that increasingly deflationary expectations raised the real interest rate and discouraged investment. One way in which a new, expansionary policy regime would affect economic activity is by reducing the real interest rate again. The De Long and Summers (1986) model used in lecture 2 (and described in appendix A) shows how this channel would operate. The model shows one way in which revised expectations affect economic activity; there is no implication that it is the only channel. In particular, expectations that demand would be expanding could stimulate investment at constant prices.

I argued also that the primary thread running through the deflationary policies of the early 1930s was adherence to the gold standard. Devaluation — going off gold in the parlance of the day — was therefore a good signal of a changed policy regime. It was not an infallible indicator, of course, as was shown by the British experience of 1931, but it was the best one available.

Devaluation also had other effects, as shown in the Eichengreen and Sachs (1986) model used in lecture 1 (and described in appendix A). The stimuli from relative prices and monetary ease were added to the effects of a changed policy regime. In fact the interaction was beneficial. Devaluation that was part of a change in the policy regime speeded the change in expectations by showing a tangible sign of the new regime. And the changed expectations that came from the initiation of a new policy regime amplified the effects of the devaluation.

This analysis can be seen as an extension of Eichengreen and Sachs'. They argued that devaluation helped the recovery of European countries, individually and in the aggregate. For each country and for the aggregate, devaluation allowed greater monetary ease. If only some countries devalued, they gained a relative price effect as well. Eichengreen and Sachs substantiated this argument by regressions for ten European countries. The United States and Germany, however, did not fit their model as tested. My analysis adds more general aspects of policy formation to their analysis of devaluation. The United

States and Germany both experienced changes in policy regimes, although only one had a devaluation.[14]

The change in policy regime can be seen most clearly in the United States.[15] The Hoover administration followed a policy regime that became more orthodox over time. It was highly traditional in its support for the gold standard and its focus on efforts to bolster the credit markets rather than the economy directly. Although not initially deflationary, Hoover drew exactly the wrong lesson from the currency crisis of 1931 and became a strong deflationist (Stein 1969, ch. 2; Barber 1985).

The Reconstruction Finance Corporation is the exception that proves this rule. Hoover's most forceful expansionary effort, the RFC was strictly limited in its goals. Hoover wanted the RFC to promote investment, but he limited the RFC to an agency function, making the its finance "off-budget" and emphasizing the "soundness" and "bankable" quality of supported projects. The RFC in addition was directed at the relief of financial institutions; two-thirds of its 1932 loans went to them (Barber 1985, pp. 130–132, 170–174). The expansionary aspect of the RFC therefore was designed to be a mild exception to the prevailing deflationary regime, not the start of a new direction.

The Federal Reserve, as discussed in lecture 2, maintained a passive stance in the early stages of the Depression, replaced by active contraction in response to the run on the dollar in 1931. The Federal Reserve's steps toward expansion in March to July of 1932 were halted when the open market purchases alarmed other central banks and threatened the solvency of member banks by lowering the returns on bank portfolios (Epstein and Ferguson 1984).

The Hoover administration's defense of the gold standard and the existing gold value of the dollar was never less than firm, even after Britain left gold. The administration was tested in this resolve in the fall of 1931, and again in February 1933. In each instance the answer was strict adherence to the existing gold value and orthodox monetary restriction. The Federal Reserve raised interest rates and accelerated the contraction in response to the loss of gold in the fall of 1931; the Glass-Steagall Act of 1932 reiterated support for the gold standard six months later. Hoover tried to make an issue of his defense of the dollar in his reelection campaign, only to have it backfire on him. As late as February 1933, Hoover spoke out against a U.S. devaluation and urged worldwide restoration of the gold standard. Echoing both the sentiments and the prescience of Benjamin Strong eight years before, Hoover declared: "The American people will soon be at the fork of three roads. . . . The third [and worst] road is that we should inflate our currency, consequently abandon the gold standard, and with our depreciated currency attempt to enter a world economic war, with the certainty that it leads to complete destruction, both at home and abroad" (Hoover 1933).

It was not clear during the presidential campaign of 1932 that Roosevelt would implement a change of policy regime. He had recently raised taxes in New York to balance the state budget, and he emphasized a balanced federal budget as well. He strongly criticized Wall Street, business, and utilities during the campaign and employed a generally antibusiness rhetoric. These were not features of a candidate one would expect to help the business environment.

The first sign that a new policy regime was on the way came after the election, in December 1932, when Roosevelt torpedoed Hoover's efforts to settle war debts and reparations multilaterally, signifying his opposition to continuation of the existing international financial cooperation. A change in regime became more tangible in February 1933, when the President-elect began a serious discussion of devaluation as part of an effort to raise commodity prices. This talk led to a run on the dollar and helped cause the Bank Holiday in March. The New York Fed found its gold supplies running dangerously low at the start of March. It appealed to the Chicago Fed for help. But the midwestern bank refused to extend a loan to its New York cousin, its different view of the world echoing the contrast between the German and French attitudes when Luther appealed for a similar loan in July 1931. The New York Fed appealed to Roosevelt to shut down the entire national banking system, a draconian way to force cooperation among the Federal Reserve banks (Wigmore 1987).

Once inaugurated, Roosevelt declared the Bank Holiday. He also imposed controls over all foreign exchange trading and gold exports. He ended private gold ownership and took control over the sale of all domestic gold production. These controls allowed Roosevelt to avoid speculative disequilibrium when he began to devalue the dollar. He did so on April 18 when he announced that he would support the Thomas amendment to the Emergency Farm Mortgage Act of 1933 which allowed him to set the price of gold. At the same time he prohibited the private export of gold by executive order. The dollar, freed from its official value, began to fall. It dropped steadily until July, when it had declined between 30 and 45 percent against the pound (Federal Reserve System 1943, pp. 662–681).

The clarity of the change in policy was unmistakable. The United States was under no market pressure to devalue. Despite the momentary pressure on the New York Fed, the United States held one-third of the world's gold reserves, ran a chronic foreign trade surplus, and dominated world trade in modern manufactures like automobiles, refrigerators, sewing machines, and other consumer durables. The devaluation was a purely strategic decision that appeared without precedent. Orthodox financial opinion recognized it as such and condemned it. Senator Carter Glass called it an act of "national repudiation." Winthrop Aldrich, the new chairman of the Chase National Bank, thought devaluation was "an act of economic destruction of fearful magnitude" (Wigmore 1985, p. 426).

This was a change of regime of the type described by Sargent in his account of the end of several hyperinflations. It was a dramatic change, clearly articulated and understood. It was coordinated with fiscal and monetary policies. The new regime clearly was designed to increase both prices and economic activity. It was supported by a wide degree of consensus—professional, public, and congressional—despite the vocal opposition of some financial leaders. The remarks by Aldrich and Glass show that the shift in regime was clearly visible. They represent, however, only a minority opinion identified with the previous, failed regime. Aldrich himself quickly joined the bandwagon and became an enthusiastic proponent of the New Deal.

Devaluation was only one dimension of a multifaceted new policy regime. During Roosevelt's First Hundred Days, the passive, deflationary policy of Hoover was replaced by an aggressive, interventionist, expansionary approach. The New Deal has been widely criticized for internal inconsistency (Hawley 1966; Lee 1982). There was, however, a steadily expansionary bias in policy that added up to a marked change from the Hoover administration. (The New Deal also turned away from the market toward a managed economy and democratic socialism, as I will explain below.)

A major step toward a compatible monetary policy was taken when Eugene Meyer resigned as chairman of the Federal Reserve Board. Meyer, an orthodox Wall Street financier with a strong international orientation, was replaced by Eugene Black, governor of the Atlanta Federal Reserve Bank, who was compliant to the wishes of the administration. The Federal Reserve cut the discount rate in both April and May from 3.5 to 2.5 percent, and its holdings of U.S. Treasury securities rose from $1.8 to $2.4 billion between April and October (Federal Reserve System 1943, pp. 343, 440). The change in monetary regime initiated by devaluation was extended by reforms of the Federal Reserve System that initiated what contemporary observers labeled a new monetary system (National Industrial Conference Board 1934).

Devaluation received wide, although not (as we have seen) universal, support. J. P. Morgan told reporters, "I welcomed the reported action of the President and the Secretary of the Treasury in placing an embargo on gold exports" (Wigmore 1985, p. 426). Keynes advised a client that, "President Roosevelt's programme is to be taken most seriously as a means not only of American but of world recovery. . . . [H]is drastic policies have had the result of turning the tide in the direction of better activity" (Keynes 1933). Congress easily passed the New Deal measures. The business and farm community welcomed the possibility of "reflation."

The reaction to Roosevelt's new policy regime was immediate. The stock market rose as the value of the dollar fell, signifying the business community's favorable reception to the new regime. Stock prices, which had been bouncing around at a low level in 1932, almost doubled in the second quarter of 1933 (Federal Reserve System 1943, p. 481). Farm prices—or at least the prices of those products like cotton and grain that were traded on international markets—rose sharply as well. These movements can be seen in figure 3.1, which compares the price of cotton in dollars with the value of the pound. It can be seen that there was little reaction in the cotton price when the pound

**Figure 3.1**
The price of cotton and the exchange rate, 1930–1936. *Solid line*:
cotton price to U.S. farmers (1909–1914 = 100); *dotted line*: value of
the pound in dollars. Source: *Survey of Current Business*
(Supplement, 1936, p. 15); Federal Reserve System (1943, p. 681).

was devalued in 1931. The devaluation of the dollar in
1933, by contrast, had immediate and spectacular effects.

Kindleberger (1986) asked why the British devaluation
lowered prices abroad while the American devaluation
raised them at home. There are two answers to this question. As noted in in figure 3.1 (and in lecture 2), foreign
prices did not fall very much after the British devaluation.
They had already dropped from the high levels of the late
1920s and were beginning to find new levels. The British
market was not big enough to derail this process. More
important, the British devaluation was a change in the
price of pounds but not a change in the policy regime of
Britain. It was the new, expansionary policy in the United
States that imparted an inflationary impulse to the world
economy.

Investment—encouraged by the new regime, by demands from the rejuvenated farm sector, and by the higher

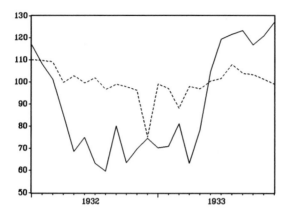

**Figure 3.2**
Indexes of investment and consumption spending, 1932–1933.
*Solid line*: investment spending; *dotted line*: consumer spending.
Source: Temin and Wigmore (1988).

stock market—began to rise. Automobile and steel production in particular posted dramatic gains in the second quarter of 1933. The results can be seen in figure 3.2, where monthly indexes of investment and consumption spending in the United States are shown. The investment series is based on orders for heavy equipment; the consumption index, on department store sales. They both embody information available more frequently than national income aggregates. It is clear that the recovery in the United States began shortly after Roosevelt's inauguration and that it was led by investment. It was a rapid response to the new policy regime introduced by the new President.

The story is similar, although not as clear-cut, in Germany. Brüning was replaced by Papen in late May 1932. The Lausanne Conference effectively ended reparations and cleared the major political hurdle from Germany's path. As I have argued in lecture 2, reparations were a far more potent political than economic factor. Their removal therefore needs to be seen also as an event that cleared the political path.

Brüning's deflation was replaced by Papen's first steps toward economic expansion. Brüning had initiated a small employment program that had little effect in the context of his deflationary policy regime. This program was expanded by Papen and complemented by some off-budget government expenditures. In addition Papen introduced tax credits and subsidies for new employment (Hardach 1980, pp. 47–48). These were steps in the right direction, but they did not alter the perception of the policy regime. They still appeared to be isolated actions, not regime shifts.

The new policy measures (like the Fed's open market purchases earlier that year) nevertheless produced some effects. There was a short-lived rise in industrial production and shipments. The recovery was only partial, and the data are mixed, but there was a definite sign of improvement (Henning 1973). These tentative results seem to have had an immediate political impact. The Nazis had leapt to prominence in the 1930 election and increased their seats in the Reichstag from 12 to 107. They then doubled their large representation in the Reichstag in the election of July 1932. But that was their high point in free elections. They lost ground in the second election of 1932, in November, garnering 33 percent instead of 37 percent of the vote and reducing their representation in the Reichstag from 230 to 196 seats (Hamilton 1982; Childers 1983).

Further economic improvement could well have reduced the Nazi vote even more. If so, we need to ask whether the recovery begun under Papen could have continued. For if it had, then the political courage to hold out a little longer with the Papen or Schleicher governments might have spared Germany and the world the horrors of Nazism. The question then is not simply about the recovery. It is also whether Germany—and hence the world—was balanced on a knife-edge in 1933 between the continuation of normal life and the enormous costs of the Nazis.

There is, however, only a slim case for believing that the recovery could have been sustained. The instability of politics mirrored the instability of the economy. The policy regime was in the process of changing, but there was no clear signal of change like the American devaluation. There was no assurance that Papen's tentative expansionary steps would be followed by others. The recovery of 1932 consequently was neither sharp nor universal. Even though a trough can be seen in some data, other series show renewed decline into 1933. The economy fell back to its low point under the brief administration of Kurt von Schleicher, and it appeared that the Papen recovery was abortive.

For Nazism to have been a transitory fad, the recovery would have had to resume in early 1933. It would have had to be strong enough to repair the damage to the political fabric caused by the "myriad social and political ramifications" of extensive unemployment (Stachura 1986, p. 21). The expansive policies already undertaken would have had to have further effects—which they probably did—and the American recovery would have had to spill over into Germany. Both factors are possible but neither would have been very strong, and the latter in addition would not have come for several months. One can argue that the future course of the German economy under elected governments would have limited the Nazis to continued minority status, but it is harder to argue that it would have led to a rapid decline in Nazi support.

Hitler was appointed chancellor at the end of January 1933, and sustained economic recovery began only thereafter. There is no agreement on the cause of the German recovery. Overy (1982, p. 28) concluded in his survey of the literature that "there is no single or simple answer." The advent of the Nazi government, however, heralded the presence—as in the United States—of a new policy regime. The literature has analyzed the economic aspects of reparations, and I have stressed their political effects. I want to do the opposite here. Instead of focusing on the clear political discontinuity in 1933, I want to expose the clear change in economic policy.

The Nazi government was truly a new (and horrible) regime, both politically and economically. The Nazis set out immediately to consolidate their power and destroy democracy. They obliterated democratic institutions. They turned away from international commitments to the restoration of domestic prosperity. And they gave their highest priority to the reduction of Germany's massive unemployment. Hitler conducted a successful balancing act. He reassured businessmen that he was not a free-spending radical at the same time as he expanded the job creation programs and tax breaks of his predecessors. The First Four Year Plan embodied many of the new measures and gave them them visibility as a new policy direction (Guillebaud 1939). ⸺

Employment rose rapidly in 1933 as a result. The new expenditures must have taken time to have their full effects. The immediate recovery was the result of changed expectations when the Nazis took power. It was the result of anticipated as well as actual government activities.[16] Even though the specifics of the Nazi program did not become clear—in fact were not formulated—until later, the direction of policy was clear. Hitler had been criticizing the deflationary policies of his predecessors for years, and the commitment of the Nazis to full employment was well known. As in the United States, a change in policy regime was sufficient to turn the corner, although not to promote full recovery.

This analysis emphasizes the role of expectations in the beginning of economic recovery. Modern theories of the economy have brought expectations onto the stage as a lead actor, unlike their earlier position as extra or under-study. Our historical accounts need to follow suit. Changing prices and specific measures were important, but they needed to form a pattern that encouraged private firms to resume production and investment. This need for a new policy regime underscores the importance of Roosevelt's and Hitler's initial actions and pronouncements. It suggests that the American parallel to Papen's expansionary measures was Hoover's RFC or the Federal Reserve open market purchases in early 1932, not one or another element of the New Deal.

Britain and France did not follow the pattern set by Germany and the United States. Britain, which had escaped the worst of the Depression by its devaluation, continued on its path of mild encouragement through easy money (Howson 1975). France clung to the gold standard and became the ideological leader of the gold bloc. Having enjoyed the benefits of an undervalued currency in the twenties, France was unable to avoid an overvalued currency in the thirties. But while the franc's undervaluation was destabilizing to the world, France alone bore the pain of the overvalued franc.

Similarity in the continuity of economic policy did not reflect parallel political histories in Britain and France any more than the reversals of policy in the United States and Germany reflected a common political direction. The National government in Britain lasted throughout the 1930s; there were eleven different governments in France between 1932 and 1936. After the conservative riots of February 6, 1934, France responded to the economic pressure from abroad in classic gold-standard form. Rather than devalue in early 1934, they deflated their economy.

More precisely, they proclaimed that they were continuing an existing deflationary policy (Jackson 1985, p. 88).

The new policy regimes in the United States and Germany were powerful enough to arrest the worldwide decline, despite the continuation of traditional policies in Britain and France. Prices and production began to rise; unemployment began to fall. But only in Germany was the expansionary impulse strong. There was not enough expansionary force in the United States and Britain to bring the world economy back to full employment.

It is not to be doubted that global full employment would have been a formidable goal in 1933. (Had it been easy, we might have expected more countries to reach it.) Expectations turned around when macroeconomic policies reversed, but they did not recapture the heady spirit of the previous boom. More important, the world economy in 1933 suffered from four years of neglect. New investment had ground to a halt in many countries, and the capital stock had been allowed to run down. With a smaller stock of capital per potential worker, there were fewer job opportunities. (This can be shown formally, as done in Blanchard 1988, and in appendix A.) The "recovery" of 1933 was a decisive change in direction, not a return to full employment.

The path of real gross domestic fixed investment in the United States and Germany is shown in table 3.1. The decline in both countries was startling. Real fixed investment in the United States was only one-quarter of its level in the late 1920s by 1933. Assuming that depreciation was a function of the capital stock, it did not fall anywhere near as much. The fall in *net* fixed capital formation consequently was even more dramatic. Net fixed investment in the United States virtually ground to a halt. Fixed investment did not fall quite so precipitously in Germany. It fell

**Table 3.1**
Gross private fixed investment

| | Nominal | | Real (1929 = 100) | |
| --- | --- | --- | --- | --- |
| Year | United States ($ million) | Germany (RM billion) | United States | Germany |
| 1927 | 14.6 | 10.3 | 101.9 | 106.6 |
| 1928 | 14.5 | 11.1 | 99.6 | 111.9 |
| 1929 | 14.5 | 10.1 | 100.0 | 100.0 |
| 1930 | 10.6 | 8.3 | 75.9 | 83.8 |
| 1931 | 6.8 | 5.0 | 52.0 | 54.2 |
| 1932 | 3.4 | 3.1 | 29.5 | 39.1 |
| 1933 | 3.0 | 3.7 | 26.3 | 47.9 |

Sources: U.S. Bureau of the Census (1975), pp. 224, 229; Swanson and Williamson (1972), p. 70; Germany (1938), pp. 318–319, 565; Balderston (1983), p. 401.

below two-fifths of its level in the late 1920s, implying that here too net fixed investment was at a very low ebb.

This does not mean that economic policy was powerless to create jobs. The Nazis set out to reduce unemployment in 1933 and 1934, and they did so. German unemployment peaked at 30 percent in 1932 and declined to 12 percent by 1935 (Mitchell 1980, p. 178).[17] The German approach, of course, was dramatically different from the American. The initial expansion of the American economy at the turning point was led by investment. But investment in Germany expanded only slightly more rapidly than in France or Britain. Table 3.2 shows the path of investment in four countries during 1932–33. Expansion in the United States, as noted earlier, was led by an investment boom. Expansion in Germany, as well as other countries, was centered in consumption. Hitler consolidated his political revolution, with an immediate economic gain to the German people.

It was a major achievement to turn the economic tide.

**Table 3.2**
Production of investment goods in selected countries (1932.III = 100)

| Country | 1932.IV | 1933.I | 1933.II | 1933.III |
|---|---|---|---|---|
| United States | 117 | 113 | 179 | 258 |
| United Kingdom | 104 | 110 | 117 | 115 |
| Germany | 105 | 100 | 128 | 135 |
| France | 101 | 109 | 120 | 121 |

Source: League of Nations (1934), p. 130.

Orthodox deflationary policies were replaced by expansionary ones in America and Germany. The change had immediate and dramatic impact on the economy. Economic expansion, however, is a goal rather than a policy. We may presume that everyone—except possibly the hapless Brüning with his obsessive desire to eradicate reparations—desired the return of prosperity. Their disagreements were on means, not ends. Deflationists thought that internal prices had to be reduced in order to reestablish prosperity. Roosevelt and Hitler rejected this view. What did they put in its place?

It was not a Keynesian model. Keynes was only one of many expansionists in the early 1930s; his intellectual dominance of economic thought would not appear until the end of the decade. Keynesian analysis, in fact, was an outgrowth of the Depression. Policymakers in the 1930s did not make the distinction that we make today between microeconomics and macroeconomics. They attributed the Depression to structural problems as much or more than to problems of economic aggregates. They consequently used a mixture of microeconomic and macroeconomic policies to try to throw off the Depression (Temin 1982).

The new policy regimes therefore were not Keynesian, either in form or substance. Brown (1956) long ago pointed out that the full-employment budget in the United States was not increased over its 1929 level in the following decade. The 1930s were not a test of Keynesian theory because Keynesian policies were not used.[18] Overy (1982) concluded that the Nazi policy regime also was not Keynesian. Milward (1983), in a review of Overy's book, signified the general agreement on this issue by responding, "But who ever said it was?"

Governments tried to take control of their economies at the same time as they tried to resuscitate them. Having seen the chaos generated by orthodox finance and relatively unfettered markets, they opted for more planning and control. The alternatives to financial orthodoxy, however, were not as well articulated as classical liberalism. Many economists in the United States and Germany had urged their governments to abandon their deflationary policies in favor of government spending and (sometimes) credit expansion. But their policy prescriptions were more coherent than their explanation of how the problem had arisen. They consequently had found it difficult to oppose the counterarguments of politically powerful deflationists (Davis 1971; Garvy 1975).

The dominant intellectual tradition that opposed classical liberalism in the early 1930s was that of socialism. It was primarily between liberal adherents of the market and socialists of various guises that the ideological battles were fought. The rules of government finance as dictated by the gold standard said that government intervention was bad, unless it was simply speeding the natural responses of the private economy. The alternative was a view that government could be an instrument to help the working man; in other words, that government participation in the economy was good (Gourevitch 1986).

It has become fashionable among historians to deny the existence of internal consistency to the new policy regimes introduced at the depth of the Depression. For example,

Milward (1977, p. 8) said that the National Socialists knew only that they were opposed to the gold standard, but lacked any positive ideas. Their economic policy "was dictated by political expediency and . . . crises." James (1986, p. 347) stated flatly, "There was nothing socialist about Hitler's economics," and went on to detail individual aims that, James said, were frequently in conflict with one another. Hawley (1966, p. 481) concluded that planning in the New Deal was "partial, piecemeal, and opportunistic." Himmelberg (1976, p. 219) found that, "The NRA resulted from the interplay of several independent political forces." Lee (1982) articulated the main stream of American historiography when he denied the existence of "any conscious design" among Roosevelt's advisors and emphasized the continuing conflicts among them.

I do not want to claim here that there was no dissension or conflict in the German or American government. I do want to emphasize the consistency that shone through the confusion. I want to assert that there was a new policy regime that was not simply noise (Garraty 1986, ch. 8). It was visible to members of the economy, where it encouraged consumption and investment that promoted economic recovery. It was ever changing as ideas and events impinged on policy, but the new regime kept its essential shape outside of Germany, where it was overtaken by Nazi ideology and war preparation. The contradictions were there, but the opposing elements were seen as deviations from the underlying policy regime, like Hoover's and Papen's isolated expansionary moves. Warts, contradictions, and all, the new policies were basically socialist.

There are many reasons to emphasize the socialist element in the efforts to introduce and expand government management of the economy. For starters, the participants in this process themselves used the term. Nazi is short for

National Socialist German Workers' Party (*Nationalsozialistische Deutsche Arbeiterpartei*). Even though the socialist wing of the Nazi party lost out in the internal power struggle and the Nazi use of the socialist label was quite cynical, Nazi policies still retained a socialist bent. And like good socialists, the Nazis poured invectives over other socialists. Roosevelt included advisors of many views in his government. Few of them dared to call themselves socialists in the American context, but their critics had no such inhibitions. A little later, Blum's Popular Front was explicitly socialist. Later still, the British Labor party implemented an avowedly socialist program.

In addition these programs all shared important socialist common elements. No sensible person would attempt to minimize the distance between the Nazis and any democratic government. National socialism is close to an oxymoron. Maier (1987, p. 71) said, "Fascism was just crisis capitalism with a cudgel." As I stated at the outset of these lectures, the interwar period is best seen as a truce in the Second Thirty Years' War. The tensions left from the first military encounter erupted in sporadic economic and military confrontations throughout the 1920s and 1930s. The ongoing conflict between the French and Germans was important in both the origin and the spread of the Depression, as I have described already. And the horrors of the Nazi regime would bring on the Second World War.

Nevertheless, there still was an impulse to take control of the economy in common ways in the 1930s. Free market capitalism and the orthodox finance of the gold standard had led to disaster. Direct management of the economy could only do better. And though there was no tight theory of a managed economy that led each country down the same path, there were ideas in the air that led them in similar directions.[19]

Finally, the socialist impulse of the 1930s surfaced after the Second World War in a more uniform pattern in Western Europe and America that often is termed the "mixed economy." Instead of dividing between socialist and liberal countries, the four countries considered here increasingly adopted similar approaches to the role of the government in the economy. The common political compromise is reflected in the neutral term, the mixed economy. The mixture, clearly, was of fiscal orthodoxy and free markets, on the one hand, and socialist control of the economy, on the other.

It is not possible to define socialism as clearly as the gold standard. I offer a definition here to distinguish socialism from other kinds of government intervention in the economy. A socialist economy has the following properties: (1) public ownership *or regulation* of "the commanding heights" of the economy, particularly of utilities and banking; (2) heavy government involvement in wage determination; and (3) a welfare state providing everyone with, in Oscar Lange's words, "a social dividend constituting the individual's share in the income derived from the capital and the natural resources owned by society" (Lange and Taylor 1938, p. 74).

This definition differs from the one used today to distinguish Eastern and Western Europe (Nove and Nuti 1972). Instead of emphasizing the ownership of assets in a formal sense, it considers ownership in the sense of having discretion over an asset (Grossman and Hart 1987). A nominal owner of an asset who cannot sell his asset and is forced to sell his output through a government agency at a government-dictated price is not much of an owner. (This is a capsule description of Nazi agriculture.) The definition used here also stresses the relation of the state to the worker, a critical part of socialist thought.

This definition of socialism distinguishes socialism from the practice of many socialist parties who had been seduced by the central bankers and the proponents of fiscal orthodoxy. In their desire to be respectable, the Labor party in Britain and the Social Democratic party in Germany were as staunch supporters of the gold standards and deflationary finance as their conservative opponents. For example, Sidney Webb, a member of the Labor government in 1931, remarked after Britain left gold, "No one told us we could do that!" (McKibban 1975; Borchardt 1984).

There is considerable room for variation within these elements of socialism. Not all socialist regimes look alike. Not all mixed economies contain all these characteristics. These properties, however, were common to socialist thought and in the movement away from a market economy in the 1930s and 1940s. They provide a guide to the shared aspects of the new policy regimes in the United States and Germany that separated the new regimes from the traditional policies in Britain and France before 1936.

These common elements also highlight the dominant problem of the 1930s. Employment opportunities in the middle of the decade were limited by the lack of investment in its early years. But this did not have to mean unemployment. Employers typically hire more workers when the ratio of wages to the price of their product fall. There consequently was a low real wage consistent with the recovery of full employment. Why didn't real wages fall to the point where employment could recover?

The reader will recall at this point the discussion of price flexibility in lecture 2. There I stated that price—and hence wage—flexibility was harmful to the stability of the economy in the early 1930s because price and wage declines generated expectations of further declines. How can I argue here that price cuts would have been stabilizing in the mid-1930s?

The answer depends on expectations, which have been incorporated into this analysis. Economic anticipations were different after 1933. The harmful effects of wage cuts in the early 1930s came from the expectation that they would continue (see appendix A). Early in 1933 the policy regimes in the United States and Germany changed, decisively putting an end to contraction and deflation. Low wages in the context of the new, expansionary policy regimes did not generate deflationary expectations. They therefore did not have dynamic effects that destabilized the economy. In the jargon of economics, the Keynes effect outweighed the Mundell effect after the first few months of 1933.

Blanchard and Summers (1986) suggested a reason why wages did not always fall when unemployment was high in the context of the high European unemployment of the 1980s. They argued that "hysteresis" in wage setting can prevent the real wage from falling enough to restore full employment. In their model wages are set to preserve the jobs of those people already employed, not to move others out of unemployment. Workers react to negative external shocks—like the deflation of the early 1930s—by accepting lower real wages, but only low enough to preserve the jobs of those still employed. The result is that the economy lacks a strong force tending to full employment. This model of the labor market can be incorporated into an IS-LM framework. (The details are shown in appendix A.) In contrast with the models presented already, this one—here in the version due to Blanchard (1988)—elaborates the determinants of aggregate supply instead of aggregate demand.

Wages were set in the socialist context of the 1930s with the active involvement of the government. I have suggested that this was one of the defining elements of a socialist regime. Another, however, was the distribution of income to all members of the economy. If wages were set low enough to provide full employment, then the redistributive impulse could be subsumed under the goal of employing all workers. But if the government set wages higher than this, if it accepted or encouraged wage setting to benefit the already employed, then the redistributive aspect of socialism had to be solved by different means.

One of the distinctive aspects of national socialism—or fascism, to use the more conventional term—was the government's identification with employers rather than workers in wage bargaining. Fascism (in both Germany and Italy) was partly a reaction to the previous high wages that were thought, at least by the business community, to have debilitated the economy (Maier 1987, p. 103). It was a reaction to the combination of high wages and fiscal orthodoxy advocated by the socialist parties. The combination, as we have seen, was insupportable.

The fascist organized destruction of unions led to low wages and the rapid recovery of employment. Under democratic socialism, by contrast, the government promoted strong unions and high wages. Policymakers then found that they had to confront directly the problems of income distribution. Although this difference in wage setting was hardly the cause of the Second World War, it underlies the differences between the way in which new political alignments expressed the socialist impulse to take control of the economy and welfare coming out of the Depression.

In fact the Nazis seized control of an economy that already had many socialist characteristics. The Weimar government was heavily involved in mediating collective bargaining for wages throughout the 1920s. The government had virtually nationalized the banks in the wake of the currency crisis of 1931 (Stolper, Häuser, and Borchardt, 1967, pp. 106–117). But the government's commitment to the gold standard had vitiated any gains from these policies, ensuring that there was no "social dividend" to distribute.

In order to stimulate recovery, the Nazis—like the Democrats in the United States—had to establish a startling new policy regime. To do so, they threw the baby out with the bathwater, destroying many of the socialist institutions of the Weimar republic. But they replaced them with their own institutions that performed the functions I have identified as socialism. Personal freedom and autonomy were sacrificed in the process of controlling production and wages and distributing the "social dividend" to the populace. As Hitler is reported to have said, "Why need we trouble to socialize banks and factories? We socialize human beings" (Hayes 1987, p. 73). The Nazis' brand of heterodox socialism provided the motive force for the German economic recovery.

The Nazis set out to reduce unemployment by a variety of complementary actions. They destroyed the unions within a few months of taking power, entrusting the job of wage bargaining to a government agent, the Nazi's labor trustee. The Nazis also introduced compulsory labor service in 1935. They used tax incentives and propaganda to convince women to leave the labor force. These measures increased the demand for labor at the same time as they reduced the labor force, dramatically lowering measured unemployment. To keep industrial peace in the face of low wages, the Nazis gave workers the right—at least in theory—to try their employers in special courts for abuse of power and exploitation of workers. At the cost of their personal liberty and higher wages, the German workers achieved some amelioration of working conditions (Hardach 1980).

Despite the absence of an investment boom at the turning point in Germany, investment and government expenditure were important in the later stages of the recovery.[20] Wages were kept low by the Nazis, and they failed to keep pace with the growth of national income. Wages fell from 64 to 57 percent of national income between 1932 and 1938. Higher taxes on wage earners meant that consumption rose even more slowly, falling from 83 to 59 percent of national income in the same six years (Overy 1982, p. 34).[21]

The sum of investment and government expenditures then rose from 18 to 41 percent of national income in this same period, a change in the composition of output that rivals the Soviet's First Five Year Plan. Productivity, however, did not rise commensurately. As in other socialist regimes, there was little incentive to innovate. In fact there were disincentives. High profits were taxed heavily. Good products that were competitive on world markets could not find outlets due to the extensive trade restrictions. The Nazis opted for exchange controls rather than devaluation in part to isolate Germany from the world economy and promote their desired autarchy and in part to exploit another tool for direct control over the economy (Overy 1982, p. 37; Hardach 1980, pp. 71–72).

The Nazi government contained members who wanted to nationalize the banks, but their view was never translated into policy. In fact the steps toward nationalization taken in the aftermath of the currency crisis of 1931 were reversed. Private banking, however, did not play the role in the recovery that it had performed in earlier German industrialization. The boom was based on heavy government expenditures, and the government financed its own programs directly, by selling bonds directly to nonfinancial firms and reserving the formal capital market for government loans. The government also granted loans to firms at preferential rates, gave subsidies, and favored internal financing. The private banking system therefore did not share in the recovery until quite late in the 1930s. Socialist control of finance was accomplished by circumventing private banks, rather than by nationalizing them (Hardach 1984).

"In the long run, the Nazis aimed essentially at an economic system which would be an alternative to capitalism and communism, supporting neither a laissez faire attitude nor total planning" (Hardach 1980, p. 66). They introduced administrative controls over investment through licensing and direct allocation of raw materials. But their brand of socialism emphasized the centralized control over economic activity rather than public ownership of firms. Instead of dispossessing private owners, the Nazis severely circumscribed the scope within which the nominal owners could make choices by currency controls, taxes on profits, and direct allocation measures of the state. This was nowhere more evident than in agriculture where farms were nominally private, although they could not be sold and their output was marketed by government cartels (James 1986, pp. 355–357). Despite the retention of private ownership, government spending rose to one-third of GNP in 1938, while private investment rose only to one-fourth of that level (Overy 1982, p. 35).[22]

Government spending did not initially mean military spending. Construction of housing and roads and the manufacture of automobiles were important sources of expansion. Hitler supported motorization both for its presumed effects on production through imitation of Henry Ford and on the working class, as shown by his enthusiasm for the Volkswagen. Only after 1936, by which time the recovery was well under way, did the Nazis turn to preparation for war. After that time, of course, government expenditure increasingly shortchanged civilian investment in favor of the military (Overy 1975, 1979; Spenceley 1979).

The American recovery under the New Deal was similar to the German expansion in its use of a socialist approach to the role of government, but it was very different in its internal dynamics. The German recovery emphasized consumption at first, only to reverse course and emphasize investment over time. The American recovery, by contrast, started with investment and went on to emphasize consumption. Germany increasingly emphasized military production; the United States did not start war production until late in the 1930s. The German economy was subject to increasing control, while the New Deal imposed many controls all at once and withdrew partially under various pressures. The Germans kept wages low and reached full employment quickly; the Americans raised wages and had to cope with continued unemployment.

Nazi policy, in other words, dealt with the final two aspects of socialism (as I have defined it) together. The distribution of the "social dividend" was accomplished by promoting full employment. The New Deal took a different route. Wages were increased under the National Recovery Administration, the Wagner Act, and programs that paid a single national wage even in rural areas, perpetuating unemployment. The government had, as a result, to find a way to let workers as a whole participate in the revived economy. This problem generated many of the differences between the First and Second New Deals.

No one can doubt that Roosevelt's first hundred days comprised a whirlwind of activity. The New Deal certainly was expansionary, or "reflationist," a term that does not seem to have lasted beyond the Depression. It also took control over the economy in a way that was unprecedented. The socialist elements in this extensive intervention can be seen in terms of the three attributes of socialism as I have defined it here.

Given the widespread belief that the stock-market boom and the subsequent collapse of the financial system was the major cause of the Depression, it was not surprising that the government moved to take control over the financial sector. The Federal Securities Act initiated government oversight of new securities, which was transferred to the new Securities and Exchange Commission in 1934. The Glass-Steagall Act of 1933 reformed the banking system in many ways. It separated deposit and investment banking, on the argument that the combination had led to bank failures.[23] It introduced federal deposit insurance to prevent bank failures from cumulating into panics (Friedman and Schwartz 1963). And it—as extended by later revisions and extensions—created a genuine central bank out of the Federal Reserve System.

Control over industry in 1933 came primarily through the National Industrial Recovery Act. This act created the National Recovery Administration which oversaw the writing and implementation of industry codes of behavior. The codes allowed a whole range of cartels to come into being with government blessing in a sharp turn away from the long-standing trustbusting impulse in America. Control over agriculture was introduced with the Agricultural Adjustment Act, normally interpreted simply as price supports but included here as part of the growing government control over prices and marketing.

The government moved to take control of the wage process as well. The NRA codes limited hours of work to forty hours a week or less and raised wages. The former measure acted to spread the work; the latter, to reduce the total amount. The process of writing industry codes and bargaining for industrywide wage scales promoted the organization of labor as much as traditional government policies had impeded it. Government support for this structural change was continued in the Wagner Act of 1935 after the NRA was declared unconstitutional. The government had intervened actively in the wage process.[24]

The change in the process of wage determination had a clear effect on the level of wages. Even though prices rose under the NRA, real wages rose as well. In terms of the first two models of appendix A, the aggregate supply curve shifted upward, raising prices and decreasing employment (for a given monetary and fiscal policy) (Weinstein 1980). In terms of the dynamic Blanchard model (also in appendix A), wages now were to be set to serve the interests of those already employed, not those who wanted to be employed. The policies established by the AFL in the 1920s of protecting existing jobs for members and resisting wage cuts in slowdowns was generalized to industry as a whole (Keyssar 1986, p. 221).[25]

Table 3.3 shows the path of real weekly earnings in manufacturing in Germany and the United States and the ratio of the latter to the former. Wages in both countries fell from their peak in 1929 to their trough in 1932 at precisely the same rate. This parallelism echoes the similar rate of deflation in the two countries, but it is remarkable in view of the well-known contrasting paths of real wages in the 1920s. Real wages in both countries started up at the same rate in 1933, but then their paths diverged. Real earnings in the United States rose faster. By 1937, just before the American recession, real earnings in the United States were 30 percent above their 1933 level, while German real earnings were only just over 10 percent higher. The Nazis had kept real earnings quite stable, while real earnings had risen rapidly under the New Deal.

The American high-wage approach therefore contrasted sharply with the low-wage program of the Nazis. The smaller gains in real wages in Germany encouraged the growth of employment, as did other Nazi policies. The combined effect of the Nazi wage and employment policies was dramatic. German unemployment fell from 30 percent to 2 percent between 1932 and 1938, while unemployment

**Table 3.3**
Real weekly earnings in manufacturing (1929 = 100)

| Year | Germany | United States | Ratio |
|------|---------|---------------|-------|
| 1924 | 64  | 96  | 1.51 |
| 1925 | 79  | 95  | 1.20 |
| 1926 | 82  | 96  | 1.17 |
| 1927 | 88  | 98  | 1.11 |
| 1928 | 98  | 100 | 1.02 |
| 1929 | 100 | 100 | 1.00 |
| 1930 | 95  | 95  | 1.00 |
| 1931 | 91  | 94  | 1.03 |
| 1932 | 85  | 86  | 1.00 |
| 1933 | 89  | 89  | 1.00 |
| 1934 | 93  | 94  | 1.03 |
| 1935 | 94  | 100 | 1.07 |
| 1936 | 96  | 108 | 1.12 |
| 1937 | 99  | 115 | 1.16 |
| 1938 | 104 | 108 | 1.05 |
| 1939 | 106 | 118 | 1.10 |

Sources: Bry (1960), p. 362; U.S. Bureau of the Census (1975), pp. 164, 169.

in the United States fell only from 24 to 14 percent in 1937, before rebounding to 19 percent in 1938 (Mitchell 1980, p. 178).[26]

It must be admitted that the 1937 recession in the United States also did not help the cause of full employment. Not the result of high wages, the recession was clearly caused by government policies that curbed demand. The Federal Reserve dramatically increased the required reserve ratio in 1936, and the federal government contracted government spending sharply after the distribution of the second veterans bonus in 1936. The result of this contractionary fiscal and monetary policy was, not surprisingly, a deep recession (Friedman and Schwartz 1963, ch. 9; Peppers 1973).

Continuing high unemployment created a problem for Roosevelt. The New Deal had turned the economy around, but it had not brought full employment. Roosevelt therefore needed to attack the third aim of socialism—the distribution of income to all—separately. The Nazis had accomplished the goal of distributing the "social dividend" by providing all men with jobs. The wages were not good, and workers could not choose their jobs to improve them, but every family had access to the earnings from employment. Not so in the United States.

The Second New Deal of 1935 was Roosevelt's response to this challenge. Turning from measures to revive the economy, Roosevelt extended the government's control over the economy to spread its output more evenly. The organization of labor under the NRA was institutionalized by the National Labor Relations (Wagner) Act and the creation of the National Labor Relations Board when the NRA was declared unconstitutional. The NLRB was only one of the many regulatory bodies established to oversee and control the economy. Utilities, in particular, were subject to regulation on a new scale. As in Germany, the scope for independent action by private owners was sharply reduced.

Various measures—rural electrification, a moratorium on farm foreclosures—extended the government's helping hand into the countryside (Rucker and Alston 1987). The Social Security Act initiated a program that would end up with the government supporting directly a major part of the population. Unable to pass legislation offering aid to the poor, the program's proponents seized on aid to the elderly as a way of getting the socialist camel's nose into the policy tent (Lubove 1986).

Herein lies a paradox. Conventional wisdom asserts that high wages raise costs and reduce international competitiveness. (This is the effect of an upward shift of the aggregate supply curve.) The American economy in the late 1930s then should have found itself with a less favorable trade balance than the Nazis. The United States should have been imposing more controls over foreign trade, while Germany was relaxing its controls. But, of course, the reverse is what we observe. The Nazis imposed ever more controls over their economy and over Germany's foreign trade, as each intervention seemed to create the need for another. The Americans passed the Reciprocal Trade Agreement Act and began to reduce tariffs, drawing back from the protectionist stance adopted under Hoover.

The paradox is deepened by American business support of the high-wage component of Roosevelt's policy. Industrialists had never been as staunch deflationists as financiers, and they supported the imposition of high wages. Their argument, never clearly stated, was that high wages promoted longer job tenure, the acquisition of job skills, and innovation. Firms engaged in exploiting new technology and active in international trade were not trying to cut costs by cutting wages. High wages and low tariffs were the keys to success in their eyes (Ferguson 1984). The U.S. economy was strong and progressive in the 1930s, while the normally innovative German economy found it increasingly difficult to export under the Nazis.

This argument resolves the paradox of high wages, but it does not fit into the models of appendix A. The last model includes technical change—making a small start in the right direction—but only as a parameter. No attempt has been made to explain the pace of technical change. There are other models in the literature, typically under the label of efficiency wages, that discuss the relationship between wages and productivity. They argue that high wages encourage effort and job commitment, particularly if the alternative is considerably less pleasant (Akerlof and Yellen 1986). They offer the possibility of unifying the explanation of high wages that came from the desires of workers with one that derives from the interests of employers. Firms in the 1930s took advantage of high wages and unemployment to choose the most desirable workers and to introduce new labor practices (Jensen 1989). The effect of efficiency wages on the American economy, however, has yet to be analyzed. The full story of America's high wage economy in the 1930s has yet to be told. (The effects of low wages in Nazi Germany, of course, were inextricably connected with the problems of a tightly controlled society and economy.)

The opportunity for a shift in France's economic policy regime came in June 1936, when the Popular Front came to power and Leon Blum became premier. He instituted paid vacations and the forty-hour week with no reduction in pay. These measures raised French costs, already high due to the overvalued franc. He then raised wages more in the Matignon agreements to end the wave of sit-down strikes that greeted his administration. These French innovations, of course, are almost the same as the labor measures introduced in America under the NRA. But they were introduced in a very different context, before rather than after devaluation. The NRA convinced Americans to invest at home; the Matignon agreements led the French to invest abroad (Sauvy 1965–72, Vol. 2, pp. 202–212, 297–307).

Blum squandered the opportunity to imitate the American devaluation from (relative) strength in an attempt to blunt criticism of this action. Just as the British five years earlier had presented themselves as victims rather than initiators, Blum thought he needed international support for his devaluation. Negotiations with the Americans and British to embed devaluation into an international agreement dragged on without resolution, forcing Blum to devalue from weakness after four months had passed. The Tripartite Agreement of 1936 did little more than provide a fig leaf for Blum (Jackson 1985, p. 204).

At that point Blum had renounced the symbol of the old regime and taken control of the wage process. He was on his way to the inauguration of a new socialist regime. He could not sustain his tenuous momentum, however. French industry did not follow the American example and invest. Mobile capital that had not already fled the country did so. Blum announced the suspension of the Popular Front program in February 1937, keeping hours and pay more or less at their new levels but abandoning hope for further economic reform. The French economy received the benefit of devaluation, but the new policy regime placed short hours and high pay before economic recovery. The expansionary gains from devaluation therefore were opposed by the short-run limiting effect of high real wages. There was no time for any long-run effect of high wages on technical change to act before the war. When the economy began to recover in 1938, it was largely due to rearmament.

The British government was even more tentative. Having experienced labor conflict and general strikes in the 1920s and abandoned the gold standard in 1931, Britain lost its taste for change. The Liberals and Labor were unable to bring support for socialist policies into a successful political coalition, and the National government maintained a semblance of fiscal and monetary orthodoxy. Britain, which had escaped the worst of the Depression, refused to promote recovery aggressively. "The National government got little thanks for [recovery], partly because it did not deserve it" (Mowat 1955, p. 432). Socialist elements appeared in the support for distressed areas and the expansion of the dole for unemployed workers (Booth

1987). But without the postwar triumph of Labor, these tentative movements would have been seen as aberrations to orthodox policy rather than foreshadowing of the new.

Britain nevertheless experienced a recovery that expanded output even though it failed to reduce unemployment below double digits before the Second World War (except in 1937). The recovery came from two factors. An external stimulus came from the recovery of world output and trade. Britain, like many other countries, gained from the expansionary regimes in the United States and Germany. An internal push came from the easy monetary policy that lowered interest rates in 1932. A housing boom began, stimulated partly by lower interest rates and partly by a flow of funds into building societies in response to an interest rate differential between consols and mortgages created in the switch to easy money (Broadberry 1987). Construction and its associated industries accounted for a full 30 percent of the change in income from 1932 to 1935 (Worswick 1984). Fiscal stimulus, as in the United States, played a limited and ambiguous role (Middleton 1981; Broadberry 1984; Middleton 1984).[27]

The Second World War gave a great boost to the socialist tendencies of the 1930s. The Nazi regime, with its dictatorship and its perversion of socialist control over the economy, was defeated and destroyed. Economic planning, which had helped the allies to victory, enjoyed a well-deserved popularity. As the Allies-reconstructed their economies and aided in the reforming of the German economy, the intertwined economies of the four countries discussed here became more uniform in their expression of socialist control. They exhibited variations on the common themes of democratic socialism and mixed economy.

For present purposes, the common elements are more relevant than the differences. In each of the countries, utilities, banking, and often heavy industry were owned or heavily regulated by the government. The scope of private action in these sectors was sharply limited. Official involvement in wage setting was considerable in all countries, ranging from the German government's reconstitution of the unions to the British unions' reconstitution of the government. Wage bargaining in all four countries was dominated by the actions of large unions supported by the government. Social legislation distributed the postwar prosperity to the whole population and even sought to compensate some groups for their sacrifices during the Depression.

The postwar economies in Western Europe and America therefore contained socialist elements, but they were mixed economies. The postwar compromise included elements of fiscal orthodoxy and socialism in a pattern that emphasized stability and growth. The division between private and public ownership varied from country to country, with Britain and the United States providing the extremes. But all of these governments took an active hand in the stabilization of economic activity and the distribution of the surplus (Gourevitch 1986).

The Labor government in Britain and the first De Gaulle government in France vastly increased the extent of government ownership in their economies. They nationalized "the commanding heights" of the economy: heavy industry, transport, banking. One-fifth of industrial production was accounted for by nationalized entities. France supplemented this movement with the initiation of economic planning. Britain complemented it with policies to equalize incomes and increase welfare, following the path of the Beveridge Report in 1942 (Lieberman 1977).

Germany already had extensive government ownership of coal, iron, and electricity production. Postwar policy initially reacted to Nazi centralization by vigorous antitrust actions directed particularly toward banks. This impulse was short-lived, and Germany turned back toward government-industry cooperation in the 1950s (Stolper, Häuser, and Borchardt 1967, p. 277). The United States started the postwar period with heavy public involvement in industry, but not with large public ownership.

The government in each country supported the active role of unions in wage determination, although with very different results. Powerful unions in France engaged firms in conflict, raising wages and augmenting the postwar inflation. By contrast, the German unions acquired a voice in firm management, leading to industrial peace and reduced demands for nationalization. The British government stabilized wages—with Trade Union Congress acquiescence—in the late 1940s. The government of the United States encouraged collective bargaining, albeit with strong limitations on union power and the purging of left-wing members from the major unions (Taft 1964).

All countries saw an expansion of social welfare programs. The extension of medical care was perhaps the most visible aspect of this movement; the British National Health Service was the flagship of the trend toward government provision of basic social services. Expanded unemployment insurance and welfare programs provided for a distribution of the social dividend and assurance that the suffering of the early 1930s would not reappear. Germany and the United States emphasized government regulation of finance and industry more than government ownership. Despite the differences of initial conditions in the various countries, "the variants of the mixed economy that crystallized after the Second World War soon began increasingly to resemble each other" (van der Wee 1986, p. 320).

As I describe these measures and tendencies, you are no doubt recalling how many of them have been reversed, repealed, or abandoned in the last decade. Margaret Thatcher and Ronald Reagan have led the way back toward an

economy relatively unfettered by democratic socialist policies. They have reduced government ownership and control over "the commanding heights" of their economies by
privatization (in Britain) and deregulation (in the United
States).

These conservative governments also have removed
government support for unionization. They each signaled
the change in government policy by a dramatic labor con-
frontation. Thatcher faced down the miners; Reagan, the
air controllers. Union membership then fell from from 58
to 52 percent of nonagricultural employees in the United
Kingdom and from 25 to 18 percent in the United States
between 1979 and 1984–85. These imprecise numbers
understate that transformation of labor conditions in both
countries. In Britain, there was also a rise in the proportion
of firms operating without unions and a fall in the proportion with closed shops or covered by collective contracts.
In the United States, the decline in the 1980s followed an
earlier retreat from a peak of close to 40 percent unionized
around 1950 (Freeman 1988).

Neither Thatcher nor Reagan has made a successful
assault on the third aspect of socialism, the distribution of
the social dividend to all. Social Security in the United
States has proved largely immune to attack; it is politically
dangerous to have even voted to delay a cost-of-living
adjustment. Threats have been issued against the various
health-related programs enacted in the 1960s, Medicare
and Medicaid, but these "entitlement programs" also have
proved to have considerable popular support. The National Health Service in Britain has been similarly threatened
during the 1980s, but it continues to provide universal
health care.

A quick comparison of two American industries may
make the point. The regulation of both industries was
greatly strengthened in the Depression, and both have set

worldwide standards for public policy in the 1980s. The two industries are telecommunications and pharmaceuticals.

The Federal Communications Commission was created in 1934 to oversee telecommunications and broadcasting. It was only one of the agencies created in the New Deal to exert government control over the economy. Its jurisdiction covered a rapidly growing utility that provided telephone service for almost the whole country. The American Telephone and Telegraph Company, which had only been regulated effectively before at the state level, became a regulated monopoly at the national level as well. It performed functions as a regulated private utility that were performed directly by the government in other countries.

The United States was then the world leader in telecommunications; AT&T was making good on its aim of providing universal telephone service in America. AT&T, of course, grew with the expansion of the industry after World War II, and other companies increasingly wanted to share in this growth. The FCC backed into deregulation by allowing competition in small parts of AT&T's business that corroded the company's monopoly position.[28] The economic, political, and legal pressure on AT&T intensified in the late 1970s, and the company agreed at the start of 1982 to divide itself up in return (it hoped) for a relaxation of regulation. The United States therefore went from a regulated monopoly in telecommunications—similar to the government monopoly in most other countries—to competition in many parts of the industry (Temin 1987).

The American model has been widely imitated, although not duplicated. Britain divided telecommunications from the post, introduced a competitive telecommunications firm, and sold British Telecom to the public. It was the first public utility to be privatized by the Thatcher government. Competition, however, has been limited to only one other firm, at least until 1990 (Vickers and Yarrow 1988, ch. 8). Other countries have not been so bold. Germany, for example, has declined to introduce competition into network telephone services—the government commission on telecommunications was evenly divided on this issue—but has begun to limit the domain of the Bundespost's monopoly (Witte 1988).

Modern drug regulation in the United States dates from a 1938 act which gave the Food and Drug Administration much expanded powers. This was one of the last acts of the Second New Deal; it was only passed at all because of a tragedy that killed a hundred people. Despite this weak beginning, drug regulation has been extended and strengthened in the postwar period to substitute administrative decisions by the FDA for the actions of the private market. This regulation, although under attack from some of the same forces that successfully introduced competition into telecommunications, has only become stronger as time has gone on. Drug companies are private—and very profitable—but they operate under tight government control today (Temin 1980).

This model too has been imitated widely. Drug regulation in other countries typically is not as strict as in the United States. As in the United States, however, the trend has been toward tighter controls. Many countries have associated themselves with American regulation by ruling that drugs that have not been approved for sale in their country of origin—often the United States—cannot be marketed in their countries either. Administrative decisions have increasingly been substituted for private choices in Europe as well as in the United States (Wardell 1978).

The contrast between these two examples is stark. It illustrates the contrast between the deregulation and privatization of "the commanding heights" of the economy and the increasing government control and activity in the areas of health and welfare. The defeat of democratic socialism has not been complete. The legislation to distribute the social dividend to all has proved irreversible (at least to date). The third aspect of socialist thought seems to be more durable than either of the first two. We are not returning to the *status quo ante* 1929. The industrial economy may be approaching similar macroeconomic conditions, but the impact of economic fluctuations on working people has been very substantially reduced.

The lessons to be drawn from this tale are, as always, diverse. The theoretical lessons concern the interaction of economics and politics. The beginning of the recovery offers strong support for the role of expectations in economic affairs and for the role of government in determining these expectations. Rational expectations, the foundation of most modern macroeconomics, do not indicate a unique equilibrium for the economy (Diamond and Fudenberg 1989). Even under the strong assumption that expectations are rational, there is room for expectations to change and for the changed expectations to affect economic behavior. Governments can choose their economic policy regime and—sometimes unknowingly—their economic equilibrium as well.

The Depression offers little hope that a change in policy regime can be quickly effected when conditions change. It required a long wait and a long economic decline before a new regime could muster the political support to be implemented. It awaited the quadrennial elections in the United States, a political revolution of the most sinister sort in Germany, and years of suffering in France. The resistance to change, we may speculate, was partly due to intellectual inertia and partly due to apprehension of the leap into the unknown required to shift the policy regime.

As described, the new policy regimes had many socialist

aspects in common. This finding suggests that socialism is preferred to capitalism in times of crisis. The Depression was as close to Marx's final crisis of capitalism as we hope to see. It did not generate a lasting new order, but rather the introduction of socialist elements into capitalism. It produced democratic socialism and the mixed economy after the Second Thirty Years' War had come to its bloody close. Disorder breeds socialism.

The longest peacetime expansion on record has produced exactly the opposite. The mixed economy has been dismantled in large part in the past decade; democratic socialism is everywhere in retreat. The controls of socialism do well when times are bad, but they inhibit progress when times are good. Order therefore breeds capitalism (Jenkins 1988).

This general view of long-run economic dynamics needs to be qualified in two important ways. First, the reversion to capitalist economies has been far from complete. The distributive aspects of socialism are very attractive to democratic societies. They may well be irreversible and immune from this oscillation in economic policy regime. If so, even temporary socialist episodes may have more lasting effects on the distribution of income.

Second, there are important differences among socialist and mixed economies. In particular, the choice of wage levels has long-run as well as short-run implications. Germany kept wages low in the 1930s, expanding employment, but impeding technical change. The United States had high wages, which promoted industrial progress at the cost of neglecting unemployment. There appears to be a trade-off between the short-run gain to employment of low wages and the long-run gain in technical progress of high wages.

Conditions in the 1980s echo those in the 1930s with a significant difference. The European countries have kept wages high and endured high unemployment, while the United States has allowed wages to erode and employment to rise (Loveman and Tilly 1988).[29] But the United States has also been losing its competitive edge; its rate of technical progress has slowed down alarmingly. Perhaps we are paying a long-run price of foregone technical change (in addition to the cost of future debt service) for the short-run prosperity under Reagan.

Historically, this account echoes contemporary stories more than recent scholarship. Instead of emphasizing continuity and intellectual origins, I have stressed the discontinuity of economic policy at the start of 1933. There have been endless analyses of individual economic policies; there has been little attention to changes in policy regimes. It is not enough to analyze, say, the effect of the NRA on wages. Business plans were sensitive to the new program both for its effects on prices and wages and for its role in signaling a new and expansive policy regime. The generally negative view of the NRA derived from the narrow view is not justified.

The New Deal as a whole, Roosevelt's policy regime, represented an aberration in American economic policy. In the depth of the Depression, the United States turned from its traditional liberalism to a form of social democracy. This social democratic impulse was broadened and deepened after the Second World War, when it was in sympathy with the policies of America's main trading partners. The U.S. economy lost some of its distinctiveness in this period by joining the trend toward democratic socialism of the industrial world (Temin 1988).

This half-century of democratic socialism in America has come to an end. The 1980s witnessed a partial return to the classical liberal separation of government and economy, albeit with a difference from the pre-Depression world. The word, "liberal," for example, has become an epithet—

the "L" word—that means exactly the opposite of its traditional use. When the Republicans accused the Democrats of being liberal in the 1988 presidential election, they meant that the Democrats were social democrats. In addition the attempt to withdraw government influence from the economy has been decidedly partial. Social programs introduced originally in the Depression remain highly popular and politically robust.

The reversal of American policy has not meant a return to American exceptionalism. The United States is again participating in a common movement of industrial countries. One can even argue—although perhaps not in the home of Margaret Thatcher—that America has been leading this transformation. That, however, is the subject for another set of lectures. Here I want only to note that the United States in the 1980s has been in step, not out of step, with its companion nations.

Finally, can we infer from this account of the Great Depression whether we can avoid a repetition in the future? To the extent that we mean the distress and poverty of the Depression, the answer clearly is yes. The social programs put in place in and after the Depression have insulated the population from the harshest effects of unemployment. There are many parallels between the unemployment of the 1930s and 1980s, but the well-being of the unemployed is not one of them.

More broadly, it is extremely unlikely that the peacetime government of a major industrial country would maintain a deflationary policy regime in declining world conditions for as long as Hoover and Brüning did so in the early 1930s. (The governments of some less developed countries have unhappily been forced to do so by the debt crisis of the last decade.) I have argued here that the Depression was due to the maintenance of a failed economic policy regime, not to structural rigidities in the interwar economy. It follows that immunity from future depressions is a function of enlightened short-run policies rather than the implication of long-run changes in the international order.

Lest we all sleep too easily, let me offer two caveats. I alluded at the end of the previous lecture to the American government's nostalgia for easier times and propensity to continue the profligate macroeconomic policies introduced under Reagan. Each of these could lead to actions that might imperil the world economy. In addition, recall that the 1930s were not truly a period of peace. The years conventionally denoted as interwar are best seen instead as a truce in the Second Thirty Years' War. The policy decisions made in that context had wartime objectives of political and military advantage, rather than the well-being of the citizenry. The interactions of France and Germany, in particular, were highly destabilizing in the 1920s and 1930s. Any predictions of economic rationality by policymakers must be conditioned on the maintenance of peace.

Under wartime conditions, even cold war conditions, policies can be formulated for reasons that have little to do with macroeconomic stability. One can even think of policies that are antagonistic to prosperity, such as Brüning's attack on reparations. If we find ourselves a few years hence occupied with military rivalries or even diplomatic contests with military adventure as a threat in the background, then we should begin to worry also about the threat of a new depression.

If there is a renewed depression—which I sincerely hope there is not—then we should expect a swing of the policy pendulum back toward socialism. Capitalism thrives during economic stability. It wilts in depression. Socialism appears to be the reverse. It fades during stability from lack of the nourishment supplied by technical change. But it flowers in depression with its support of economic planning and distribution of the social dividend.

This anticipated oscillation of capitalism and socialism, like that between fixed and flexible exchange rates discussed in the last lecture, is a matter of academic interest. With any luck, it will remain in the ivory tower. These lectures have stressed the interaction of economics and politics. It is an appropriate conclusion to assert that the key to prosperity is peace.

# Appendix A:
# Underlying Models

This appendix describes the models underlying the discussion in the lectures. These models are cited where relevant in the lectures and can be found in the literature. A unified exposition is provided here to expose the common elements of these models to those who might otherwise find the different notations and expositions confusing. This appendix is written for the student who has taken or is taking an intermediate macroeconomics course. It presumes familiarity with the basic IS-LM model, which is the starting point here.

This exposition reveals also how these models can be seen as articulations of different parts of a unified general model. Although it would not be hard to write out such an overall model, it would be too unwieldy to work with. We do better to restrict ourselves, as Solow (1985) recommended, to partial models. But it is comforting to show that the models are consistent with each other.

The description of these models is organized as a theme and variations. The theme is the familiar IS-LM model, and the variations introduce, in turn, international trade, expectations, and capital formation. They are due to Eichengreen and Sachs (1986), De Long and Summers (1986), and Blanchard (1988). (They all also, coincidentally, originated in Cambridge, Massachusetts.)

The variables are expressed in logarithms, which are symbolized by lowercase letters. Where levels are discussed, capital letters are used. Constants are ignored, and coefficients are simplified by a change of units where this clarifies the argument. The notation has been unified to facilitate comparisons of the models.

The basic IS-LM model consists of an IS and an LM curve. The IS curve shows the locus of equilibrium in the goods market, where spending depends negatively on the interest rate and other factors. It can be represented as follows:

$$y = x - bi, \tag{1}$$

where $y$ is (the log of) real income, $i$ is the (the log of) the interest rate, and $x$ is a general variable representing various fiscal influences: autonomous spending, government purchases, expenditure shocks.

The LM curve shows the points of equilibrium in the money market. The demand for money is derived from the definition of velocity, $V = M/PY$, and the assumption that velocity is a function of the interest rate. Taking the log of the definition and substituting for velocity yields

$$m - p = y - hi. \tag{2}$$

The supply of money is exogenous in the simplest IS-LM model:

$$m = \bar{m}. \tag{3}$$

Equations (2) and (3) can be combined to form an LM curve. All three equations can be combined to form an aggregate demand curve. An aggregate supply curve is needed to complement the treatment of aggregate demand. The simplest model makes the supply of goods a negative function of the real wage:

$$y = -\frac{1}{a}(w - p). \tag{4}$$

Then a simple Keynesian wage determination—fixed nominal wages—closes the model:

$$w = \bar{w}. \tag{5}$$

These five equations define the basic model. It is instructive to calculate two additional equations from them. Equating money supply and demand eliminating the interest rate in equations (1) through (3) yields

$$y = \left(1 + \frac{h}{b}\right)^{-1}[(\bar{m} - p) + \left(\frac{h}{b}\right)x].$$

Ignoring the constant and redefining the units of x to make its coefficient equal to one gives an aggregate demand curve,

$$y = \bar{m} - p + x. \tag{6}$$

Aggregate demand is affected by changes in the real money stock and by other shocks. Neither of these influences is modeled explicitly in the basic model.

Equating the demand and supply for labor and rearranging equation (4) gives a price-setting equation:

$$p = \bar{w} + ay. \tag{7}$$

Prices are marked up from wages, with the margin depending on the level of income. Since the labor market is so simple, this model places its emphasis on prices. More complex models of supply start from wage-setting and price-setting equations, (5) and (7), rather than the aggregate supply equation, (4).

The first variation is due to Eichengreen and Sachs (1985), spelled out in Eichengreen and Sachs (1986). Their model expands the basic framework by introducing another country. Even though the two countries are assumed to be identical, this immediately doubles the number of equations. In addition some equations need to be modified to encompass international interactions. The goods market and the money market are the ones affected directly.

The fiscal variable, $x$, in equation (1) is replaced by a term showing the dependence of domestic demand on the real exchange rate. G is the number of ounces of gold per unit of currency. The exchange rate, E, equal to the number of units of foreign currency per unit of home currency, is equal to $G/G^*$. (Foreign variables are marked with an asterisk.) The real exchange rate is $EP/P^*$ or $GP/G^*P^*$. Domestic demand depends negatively on the real exchange rate, so the IS curve (in logs) is

$$y = -d(g + p - g^* - p^*) - bi. \tag{8}$$

The balance of payments affects the money market as well as the goods market, and the money-supply equation, (3), needs to be replaced by a function that makes the money supply endogenous. Let $R$ be the size of gold reserves in the home country. Then $R/G$ is the value of domestic gold reserves in the home currency. The ratio of $R/G$ to $M$ is the degree of gold backing of the currency, $V$, which is taken to be a policy instrument. The supply of money is then

$$m = r - g - v. \tag{9}$$

The rest of the basic model, the demand for money, aggregate supply, and the assumption of constant nominal wages—equations (2), (4), and (5)—are used without change. There are, of course, ten equations instead of five, as there are two countries. Even so, additional equations are needed to determine the additional variables, $r$ and $r^*$. Assume that international capital markets are perfect.

Then interest arbitrage will equalize home and foreign interest rates:

$$i = i^*. \tag{10}$$

Then assume that world gold supplies are fixed. One country's gain of gold, $dR$, must be offset with the other country's loss, $-dR^*$. Since $dr = d\log(R) = dR/R$,

$$s\,dr + (1 - s)dr^* = 0, \tag{11}$$

where $s = R/(R + R^*)$.

There are several interesting features of this first model. It is very close to the basic IS-LM model. It considers an open economy and specifies the money-supply process, but it does not disturb the basic structure of the model. Aggregate demand is the source of instability. There are, however, no dynamics; this is a model for comparative statics. It assumes that the equilibrium is stable and that changes in the exogenous variables lead to an equilibrium in a relatively short time.

Fiscal variables do not appear in this model. There is no exogenous element in spending. It is a function of relative prices and the interest rate. One could add a variable like $x$ in equation (1) to equation (8). It would carry through into aggregate demand without changing the effects of other exogenous variables. One could also allow the trade balance to depend on income in the home and foreign country, as in the marginal propensity to import. This complicates the analysis without changing the qualitative results.

The relation between the trade balance and aggregate demand, however, is quite different than in the simple Keynesian model. In that model, if both countries initiate commercial policy that inhibits trade, then the loss of demand decreases income in both countries. In this model, by contrast, simultaneous policies only affect relative prices. The foreign demand would in each country be reallocated toward domestic goods, not extinguished. Demand is a function of relative prices in this model, and there is no loss of efficiency from a redirection of trade. The model can be adapted to the analysis of commercial policy, but it will show small effects (Eichengreen 1989).

In fact there is no explicit balance of trade in the model. The connection between the trade balance and reserves is through the demand for money, not the balance of payments. A high domestic price leads to a high demand for imports. Domestic production is lowered, decreasing the demand for money. The higher price also decreases real balances. Gold flows in or out depending on the balance of these two forces.

The model can be solved explicitly to expose the comparative statics of policy changes. The solutions do not describe the immediate effects, which depend on the dynamics of the system, but rather the effects once a new equilibrium has been reached. The following discussion is based on explicit solutions of the model.

The first policy variable to consider is $V$, the gold backing of the currency. If a country decides to increase this backing, that is, to raise $V$, this action decreases the domestic money supply. The lowered money supply then decreases income and prices and raises the interest rate. Demand in the other country falls as well. The lowered world money supply raises world interest rates, depressing demand in both countries. The fall in prices in the home country in addition diverts demand to home rather than foreign production.

The second policy variable is $G$, the gold price of currency. Devaluation lowers $G$, but an additional decision needs to be made to close the model. The devaluing country has to choose either to avoid gold flows ($dr = 0$) or to keep the gold backing of the currency stable ($dv = 0$). Assume first that the devaluing country keeps gold from flowing out to the foreign country, a "sterilized" devaluation. The domestic money supply increases as a result of the rise in the value of the gold reserves. Prices rise, moving the economy out on its supply curve. The interest rate falls, increasing aggregate demand. And the relative price of home goods falls, $-dg > -dp$, allocating demand toward domestic production.

The money supply in the foreign country, however, does not increase because there is no gold outflow from the devaluing country. The lower interest rate increases aggregate demand, but this is offset by the diversion of demand from the foreign to the home country through relative prices. Foreign demand therefore decreases. This is a beggar-thy-neighbor policy.

These policies describe well the conditions at the end of the 1920s. The United States and France accumulated gold reserves. They did not expand production or permit inflation proportionate with the growth in their reserves, and the gold backing of their currencies consequently grew. France in addition had devalued its currency. It did not experience gold outflows. Quite the contrary, it imported large quantities of gold, beggaring its neighbors. The United States accumulated more gold, but France in addition devalued. Both were highly deflationary.

Consider now an unsterilized devaluation. The home country devalues ($dg < 0$), keeping the backing of its currency stable ($dv = 0$). As before, the effect on the home country is expansionary. But unlike the previous case, the effect on the foreign country is ambiguous. If gold does not flow out, then the devaluation beggars the neighbors as before. But if gold does flow out, then the expansionary effect of an increased foreign money supply outweighs the depressing effect of the relative price change. Both countries share in the added demand created by revaluing the home country's gold reserves. (Fiscal expansion in one country also has international repercussions that depend on the associated monetary policy.)

If both countries devalue, of course, both countries benefit. The increased reserves lead to an expanded world money supply. There is no change in relative prices, since $dg = dg^*$, and demand is not diverted from one country to the other. The joint devaluation is nothing short of a world monetary expansion. (Recall, however, that this model abstracts from the dynamic problems of a world devaluation. This will be treated in the second model.)

This case describes events in the early 1930s. Britain devalued in 1931. The United States devalued in 1933. They each proceeded to build up their gold reserves, beggaring their neighbors. But had all the major countries devalued at that time, the depression would have been ameliorated by the resultant monetary expansion. It might even have been arrested sooner than it was (Eichengreen and Sachs 1985).

The model is, of course, an abstraction. It does not aspire to a complete historical description of events, only to demonstrate their underlying logic. For example, the model as written does not explain well the events in the United States. A more articulated model is needed because the comparative static approach of this first model cannot deal with the timing of events and changes in expectations. A more expanded model is required to differentiate between the devaluation of the pound in 1931—at the point when the Depression might have been aborted by a general devaluation—and of the dollar in 1933—after production had continued to decline for an additional two years (Temin and Wigmore 1988).

The second model, due to De Long and Summers (1986), has dynamics as its focus. It therefore complements the first model by approaching the historical reality from a different direction. It is too difficult, however, to build complex dynamics onto the already complicated model one. The second model therefore takes its cue from the basic IS-LM model and modifies it in a different direction. This second model, like the first, modifies the IS curve. But instead of replacing the fiscal variable, $x$, with a more complex expression, this model modifies the interest rate term. Only in a static model can the distinction between the real and nominal interest rate be ignored. In a dynamic approach it is necessary to distinguish between the nominal interest rate in the demand for money and the real interest rate in the demand for goods.

It is not hard to modify equation (1) in this direction. The real interest rate is the nominal rate minus the expected rate of inflation. Accordingly, we need only add the expected inflation rate to the equation to get

$$y = x - b(i - [Ep_{+1} - p]). \tag{12}$$

The fiscal variable, $x$, is again a simplified representation of complex influences, in this case taken to be serially correlated. The expectational operator, $E$, is the expectation in this year of prices in the next year.

The demand for money is standard, equation (2), but the supply of money is endogenous. Like the first model, the second model removes money as an exogenous source of disturbances, although not as a transmission mechanism. But where the supply of money was a central aspect of the first model, it is only a minor part of the second. Accordingly, the monetary authority is assumed to follow an interest rate rule,

$$m = ji. \tag{13}$$

This assumption removes money as an independent influence on aggregate demand. Combining equations (2), (12), and (13) yields

$$y = \frac{1}{1+b'} [x - b'p + b(Ep_{+1} - p)],$$

where $b' = b/(h + j)$. As before, redefine the constant and the units of $x$ to get

$$y = x - p + b''[Ep_{+1} - p]. \tag{14}$$

Comparing this equation with equation (6) shows how aggregate demand has been modified in this second model. Money has been eliminated. In its place is the expected inflation rate, acting through its effect on the anticipated real interest rate.

The supply side is modified also to allow for persistent fluctuations of output in response to demand shocks. De Long and Summers incorporated Taylor's (1979) model of wage contracting into their model. Taylor assumed that wages were set by two-year contracts, with half the labor force negotiating new wages each year. The price equation is a simple markup over wages, allowing for the effect of the two-year staggered contracts:

$$p = 0.5(w + w_{-1}), \tag{15}$$

where $w_{-1}$ indicates last year's wages. Comparison with equation (7) shows that the markup over wages no longer is affected by the level of demand. In the basic IS-LM model the wage equation was simple and the price equation contained the economic content. In this model, like most current models, the price equation is simple and the economics are contained in the wage equation.

The wage equation follows the pattern of the price-setting equation (7) of the basic IS-LM model. It assumes that wages are set equal to the wages in surrounding periods with an adjustment for the level of demand. More precisely, the first element is that current contract wages are set equal to the average of wages from the contracts that overlap this one. The wages from next year's contract, of course, can only be the expected wage, since they are still unknown. The level of demand is taken to be the average of income this year and next year's income. Both of these magnitudes are only expected at the time of the wage negotiations, which are assumed to take place before this year's income is known. The resulting equation is

$$w = 0.5(w_{-1} + Ew_{+1}) + k(0.5Ey + 0.5Ey_{+1}). \qquad (16)$$

There are two benefits in moving from equation (7) to equation (16). The process underlying the wage equation can be specified in terms of bargains between rational workers and employers. In addition the use of overlapping wage contracts allows shocks to the economy to persist for more than a year. The disturbances in this model, however, still come from variations in aggregate demand. This second model, in other words, spells out some possible dynamics for the basic IS-LM model.

Unlike the first model, the interest in this model is in its approach to equilibrium, not in the resting place of the economy. Models of comparative statics can be differentiated and described in terms of partial derivatives. Models of dynamics need to have the path of the economy described. Phase diagrams or, in this case, simulations are the tools used.

De Long and Summers imposed rational expectations on their model. They required expectations to be such as to make the solution algorithm converge, but they did not attempt to describe a historical path of expectations. The solutions of the model therefore represent the results of assuming that the economic actors understood the model, not the implications of any actual expectations. I will describe their results, but I will rely on a more realistic form of expectations in my analysis.

In this second model a shock to aggregate demand is

magnified by price flexibility. A decrease in demand, for example, leads to expectations of a price decline, which raises the expected real interest rate and chokes off spending. For most values of the model's parameters, greater price flexibility increases the effects of a given shock. De Long and Summers (1986, p. 1037) note, however, "that price flexibility increases the variance of output not by increasing the persistence of shocks, but by front-loading their effects." This model illuminates the interaction between deflation and depression; it cannot explain the persistence of the Great Depression.

As explained in lecture 2, contemporary observers did not anticipate that the Depression and deflation would continue at first. They did not anticipate a continuing discrepancy between the nominal and real interest rates. They did not have rational expectations. This model consequently does not describe the opening stages of the Depression.

Price flexibility became important in the Depression as consumers and investors came to expect the deflation to continue. Deflationary expectations may well have precluded recovery in late 1930 and early 1931, although it is hard to date the turnaround of expectations. The international monetary collapse in the summer of 1931, and the deflationary policies instituted in response to them, must have reinforced deflationary expectations and intensified the reaction to the monetary shocks. The persistence of the Depression, in other words, was not due to the internal dynamics of a macroeconomic model. It was due, instead, to a sequence of deflationary shocks, whose impact was magnified by the price flexibility of the time.

Changing expectations were important in the recovery as well, as shown in lecture 3. The shift from deflationary to expansionary policies in the United States and Germany in 1933 had immediate effects on expectations. As people changed from deflationary to inflationary expectations, the anticipated real interest rate dropped, leading to an expansion of economic activity. Even though the policy measures had direct effects on production and investment, the change in expectations was the key to the start of recovery. The first two models emphasize variations in aggregate demand, much as the basic IS-LM model does. The third model, due to Blanchard (1988), emphasizes aggregate supply. It therefore simplifies the demand side to focus attention on supply.

Aggregate demand is taken to be just

$$y = x - p, \tag{17}$$

where $x$ represents both monetary and fiscal shocks. In other models, aggregate demand has been written as

$$y = m - p.$$

Equation (17) is meant to be more general than this formulation, to include both fiscal and monetary shocks. It therefore is essentially the same as equation (6), the simplified aggregate demand curve derived from the basic IS-LM model. This third model, therefore, is consistent with the demand side of the basic model and its extensions in the first two models.

The third model, with its truncated demand side, focuses attention on supply. As in the previous models the supply side is characterized by two equations. And as in the second model the supply side is modeled as a price-setting and a wage-setting equation.

Unlike the previous models which assumed competitive conditions, the third model assumes that firms are monopolistically competitive. Following the formulation of Dixit and Stiglitz (1977), all firms and all products are assumed to be symmetric, making it is possible to move back and forth between representative commodities or firms and the economy as a whole. Each product is assumed to be produced by a production function of a Cobb-Douglas type. The production function for each firm can be solved for the (log of the) labor-capital ratio, $n_i - k_i$, as a function of the efficiency corrected output-capital ratio,

$$n_i - k_i = a(y_i - k_i - q_i), \qquad a > 1,$$

where $q$ is total factor productivity and $a$ is a simple function of the elasticity of output with respect to labor. Since all firms are alike, this relation holds true for the economy as a whole:

$$n - k = a(y - k - q). \tag{18}$$

A price-setting formula for the representative firm can be derived from the assumption of profit maximization. Assuming again that all firms are alike yields a price-setting equation for the economy as a whole,

$$p - Ep = s[(a - 1)(Ey - k - q) - q + (Ew - Ep)], \tag{19}$$

where $s$ is a constant depending on $a$ and the elasticity of demand for each commodity. Since firms set prices before they know the price level, output, and the real wage, prices are set on the basis of expected quantities.

The important aspect of equation (19) for this discussion is that the capital stock enters into price formation. Instead of a constant markup over wages or an ad hoc adjustment according to the level of demand, price setting is derived from profit-maximizing behavior. Since firms' costs depend on their capital stock, the capital stock enters the price-setting equation.

The effect of capital can be seen by assuming that the economy is in an equilibrium where all expectations are fully realized. Setting expected quantities equal to their actual value and substituting from (18) into (19) gives the equilibrium relation between the real wage and the level of employment,

$$w - p = q - b(n - k), \tag{20}$$

where $b = (a - 1)/a$. The level of employment is determined relative to the capital stock, not the labor force. A shortage of capital reduces the demand for labor at any given real wage. There is no tendency toward the full employment of labor. During the Depression, investment ground to a halt. The capital stock grew little if at all for several years. The population, and therefore the labor force—or at least the labor force at constant wages—continued to grow. The result was that when recovery came, the same real wage as before led to employment of a smaller fraction of the labor force because of the scarcity of capital. Part of the explanation for the high unemployment rates in the recovery of the 1930s therefore was in the legacy of lost investment during the contraction.

Low capital stocks are only part of the explanation. Real wages could have fallen to reduce unemployment. Equation (20) does not indicate a unique relation between employment and the capital stock. It indicates only that this relation is dependent on the real wage. A wage-setting equation is needed to close the model and explain why wages did not fall in the 1930s to clear the labor market.

Continue to assume that the economy is in equilibrium. Then equation (20) can be combined with equations (17) and (18)—aggregate demand and the production function—to get a derived demand for labor,

$$w = x - n. \tag{21}$$

This is an extremely simple result. Equation (20) shows that in equilibrium, *real* wages are set by the relation between employment and capital. This equation says that *money* wages are responsive to employment and shifts in aggregate demand. A negative movement in aggregate demand, $x$, decreases either nominal wages or employment. From (20), this implies that $p$, $q$, or $k$ must also fall. It is not possible from these equations to say which will fall, whether real wages will fall (no change in $p$) or output ($q$ falls) or employment ($k$ falls). There needs to be an added determination either of the nominal wage or of the level of employment.

These are comparative static results. We have assumed away the dynamics of this third model and solved it like the first model. Now we have to leave the equilibrium and reintroduce some dynamics. Like the second model, the interest is in the dynamic movements of the economy. But we will not introduce all of the model's dynamics. For simplicity, continue to assume that firms are in equilibrium; unlike the second model, the dynamics here are in the labor market.

Assume that wages are set by some group of workers, which could be all workers or some part of the work force. Assume further that this group chooses the wage to keep its members employed. It matters then how group membership is determined. At one extreme it could be the entire labor force, $n^*$. At the other extreme, it could be limited to those workers employed last period. The range between these poles can be expressed by the following expression:

$$n_{-1} + d(n^* - n_{-1}),$$

where $d = 1$ corresponds to the former case and $d = 0$ to the latter.

Assume that this group does not know the level of aggregate demand at the time it negotiates its contracts. It seeks a wage that sets expected employment equal to its membership, where expected employment is given by equation (21) with $x$ replaced by $Ex$:

$$w = Ex - [n_{-1} + d(n^* - n_{-1})]. \qquad (22)$$

This wage can be substituted back into equation (21) to get, after adding $n^*$ to both sides, the behavior of actual unemployment,

$$n^* - n = (1 - d)(n^* - n_{-1}) - (x - Ex). \tag{23}$$

"All the dynamics of unemployment come from membership effects," as Blanchard (1988) remarks. If $d = 0$, that is, if membership is restricted to those workers employed last period, then unemployment follows a random walk. It is responsive to unexpected demand shocks, but there is no tendency for wages to move to reduce unemployment. Wages fall in response to falls in aggregate demand to reduce real wages and preserve the existing level of employment. But they do not fall enough to reestablish full employment. Nor, of course, do they fall enough to offset additional deflationary shocks.

To the extent that this membership rule describes the behavior of labor in the 1930s, unemployment was the product of both supply and demand influences. The contractionary shocks to aggregate demand—described in the first two models and summarized here only in movements of $x$—reduced employment. It also reduced the growth of the capital stock in a process not modeled here. As the capital stock fell relative to the labor force during the Depression, the reduced capital stock reduced the demand for labor at the existing real wage. Labor responded by accepting lower wages only to the extent that last year's employment was expected to be maintained. There was no pressure from labor to reduce wages to increase employment beyond this point. Movements of demand reduced employment; given the lack of investment in the early 1930s and the resultant fall in $k$ relative to $n^*$, the failure of real wages to fall prolonged the unemployment.

The third model concentrates attention on the supply side. Aggregate demand is present in only a rudimentary

**Table A.1**
Theoretical models for the Depression

| Model | (0) | (1) | (2) | (3) |
|---|---|---|---|---|
| IS | $y = x - bi$ | $y = -d(p + g - p^* - g^*) - bi$ | $y = x - b(i - [Ep_{+1} - p])$ | — |
| LM | $m - p = y - hi$ | Same | Same | — |
| MS | $m = \bar{m}$ | $m = r - g - v$ | $m = ji$ | — |
| AD | — | — | — | $y = x - p$ |
| P | $p = w + ay$ | Same | $p = 0.5(w + w_{-1})$ | $p = EP + s[(a - 1)(Ey - k - q) - q + (Ew - Ep)]$ |
| W | $w = \bar{w}$ | Same | $w = 0.5(w_{-1} + Ew_{+1}) + 0.5k(Ey + Ey_{+1})$ | $w = Ex - [n_{-1} + d(n^* - n_{-1})]$ |

form. Nevertheless, all three models are consistent with each other. They are presented in a common format in table A.1. The first two models expanded the determinants of spending to reflect international price differentials and price expectations. A demand specification including these elements could be added to this model of the supply side. This expanded model, however, would be exceedingly difficult to use and interpret. It was necessary to make a variety of simplifying assumptions to discuss the models as they stand; more complex models are much harder to manipulate.

The integration of these models needs to be informal. They can be regarded as descriptions of the same reality from different points of view. But it is not illuminating to try and formalize the entire picture. As Solow (1985) emphasized, each model has to be treated rigorously, but the attempt to create a single model for economic history is self-defeating. Our knowledge is still at the stage where we have to extend the basic IS-LM model in one direction at a time, only making sure that the separate explorations do not fight with each other.

These three models, then, provide tools for an understanding of the macroeconomics of the Great Depression. They can all be regarded as extensions of the basic IS-LM model, and they come together to provide the framework for these lectures.

# Appendix B:
# Underlying
# Regressions

This appendix reports the regressions underlying the discussion of Friedman and Schwartz's (1963) first banking crisis in the text. They argued that the rate of growth of the money supply was decreased at that time. Bernanke (1983) added that the "cost of credit intermediation" rose. These claims are tested in turn.

Table B.1 reports regressions on the monthly rate of growth of M2. It is hypothesized that the rate was a constant except for the effects of the monetary events noted by Friedman and Schwartz. Dummies were introduced at the dates noted by them. (Moving the dates by a month or so does not affect the results.) Once set to one, the dummies stay there, so each dummy captures the change from the preceding period, not from the base period.

The first regression starts after the stock-market crash and ends before Britain went off gold. It is confined to the first phase of the Depression. The dummies test for changes in the rate of growth of the money stock at the first two of Friedman and Schwartz's banking crises. They have the right sign, but they are not significantly different from zero. There was enough variation in the monthly rate of growth of the money stock that the rates following the crises could not be distinguished from those before. We

**Table B.1**
Regressions on the monthly growth rate of M2

| Period | 30.01–31.08 | 30.01–32.12 | 28.01–32.12 | 24.01–32.12 |
|---|---|---|---|---|
| C | −0.0019 | −0.0019 | 0.0001 | 0.0024 |
|  | (0.0026) | (0.0028) | (0.0023) | (0.0012) |
| FS1 | −0.0032 | −0.0032 | −0.0052 | −0.0075 |
|  | (0.0044) | (0.0046) | (0.0063) | (0.0049) |
| FS2 | −0.0041 | −0.0041 | −0.0041 | −0.0041 |
|  | (0.0048) | (0.0050) | (0.0079) | (0.0064) |
| FS3 |  | −0.0123 | −0.0123 | −0.0123 |
|  |  | (0.0046) | (0.0073) | (0.0059) |
| FS4 |  | 0.0160 | 0.0160 | 0.0160 |
|  |  | (0.0042) | (0.0066) | (0.0053) |

Source: Friedman and Schwartz (1963).
Notes: The dependent variable is the change in the log of M2. The independent variables are dummies that change from zero to one at the dates given by Friedman and Schwartz for the banking events: 30.10, 31.03, 31.09, 32.04. Standard errors are in parentheses.

can reject the hypothesis that the rate of change of the money stock changed at these dates.

The remaining regressions in table B.1 examine longer time periods to ensure that this result does not derive from the shortness of the first phase of the Depression. The second regression extends the period forward, looking at both the first and second phases of the Depression. The results are striking. The coefficients of the first two dummies are exactly the same as before; the standard error of the coefficients, scarcely different. Their lack of significance is confirmed.

The third and fourth dummies show that this finding is not due to noise in the money stock but rather to the small effect of the first two banking crises. When Britain went off gold in September 1931, the rate of growth of the money stock fell sharply. The change shows up as a significant coefficient on the third dummy. When the Federal Reserve began its open-market purchases in April 1932, the rate of growth of the money stock rose again. This change too shows up as a significant coefficient on the appropriate dummy. The third regression extends the period back to the beginning of the Federal Reserve's contractionary policies in 1928. The regression is the same as before, however, except for the first two coefficients. The rate of growth of the money supply was larger in the base period, making the coefficient of the first dummy larger by the same amount. None of the other coefficients change, since they show changes from the preceding period. The coefficient for the first banking crisis, however, fails to exceed its standard error even so.

The final regression extends the period back to 1924. The rate of growth of the money stock was positive from 1924 to 1930, as seen by the first coefficient. The coefficient of the first dummy is larger as a result but still only about 1.5 times its standard error. Even with this long and favorable period for comparison, the effect of the first banking panic on money growth was barely visible. The hypothesis that the the first banking crisis had no effect cannot be rejected with any confidence.

Bernanke proposed that the first banking crisis had its effect through the "cost of credit intermediation," not the growth of the money stock. As noted in the text, he argued that the increase in the cost of credit intermediation affected small companies and consumers far more than large firms. It should therefore have had differential effects within the economy. The proper test of this hypothesis therefore is a cross-sectional test, not the time-series tests performed by Bernanke. The fall in production in different industries should be related to the characteristics of firms in those industries.

**Table B.2**
Coefficients from cross-section regressions on industrial production

|                          | Dependent variables | | |
| ------------------------ | ----------- | ----------- | ----------- |
|                          | G31         | G33         | G38         |
| Independent variables    |             |             |             |
| CI23                     | 0.080       | 0.125       | 0.339       |
|                          | (0.138)     | (0.316)     | (0.329)     |
| CI34                     | 0.121       | 0.225       | 0.143       |
|                          | (0.180)     | (0.401)     | (0.415)     |
| CI50                     | 0.003       | 0.006       | 0.007       |
|                          | (0.002)     | (0.004)     | (0.003)     |

Sources: Federal Reserve System (1940); Thorp and Crowder (1941); Nutter and Einhorn (1969).
Notes: Entries are coefficients and their standard errors from univariate regressions. The $R^2$'s are very low; the corrected $R^2$'s, often negative. The number of observations is 13 for CI23 and CI50, and 15 for CI34.

Table B.2 reports the results of cross-sectional regressions that attempt to characterize the pattern of industrial decline over different time periods. To ensure conformity in the measured rate of change of the various industries, the components of the Federal Reserve's Industrial Production Index (seasonally adjusted) have been used. They correspond roughly to two-digit SIC industries.

The firms in the industries are characterized in two ways. The first two indexes are based on the concentration ratios of firms in the industries. Concentration ratios here are used as indexes of size rather than of market power. Specifically, the measures are the proportion of value added produced by industries in which the concentration ratios were greater than some value in 1937. There are two indexes, corresponding to $\frac{2}{3}$ and $\frac{3}{4}$, labeled CI23 and CI34, respectively. A third measure, CI50, is the proportion of output produced by the top 50 firms in the economy. The products of the largest 50 firms were divided among industries for this purpose.

The decline in production is measured on a quarterly basis in seasonally adjusted data. I examined three time periods. The first two look at the aftermath of the first banking crisis at the end of 1930. They look at decline immediately after the crisis up until Britain left gold in September 1931 and over the whole contraction. The first index then is the difference between the log of seasonally adjusted production in the fourth quarter of 1930 and in the third quarter of 1931. The second index is the difference between the fourth quarter of 1930 and the first quarter of 1933. For comparison, the change in the 1937 recession is used as a third index. It records the magnitude of the production decline between the third quarter of 1937 and the fourth quarter of 1938. This third variable allows comparison with a decline without banking crises. The three variables are called G31, G33, and G38.

The coefficients and their $t$-statistics from bivariate regressions are shown in table B.2. Almost all of these coefficients were not significantly different from zero, and the $R^2$'s of the regressions were very low. Bernanke's hypothesis is not confirmed. In fact all of the regressions have the wrong sign! They are uniformly positive. More concentrated industries and industries where the largest 50 firms were important appear to have suffered the largest declines in production.

It is worth noting that the results for the Great Depression and for the 1937 recession are indistinguishable. This suggests that the pattern of decline was similar in the two contractions. This suspicion is confirmed. The two measures from the Great Depression had a correlation coefficient of 0.93, as might be expected. They also each had a correlation coefficient with the third measure of about 0.75. The pattern of industrial decline was very similar in the Great Depression and in the 1937 recession. The allocation of industrial decline, in other words, was largely independent of the financial conditions of the early 1930s (and also of the magnitude of the decline). The role of the "first banking crisis" is again hard to see.

# Notes

1. Brown continued: "It is equally impossible to say that any country maintained it [the gold standard] in its full integrity." The issue here, however, is not the purity of the gold standard but rather its hold on people's minds. Brown was cognizant of the difference. Despite the previous statement, he asserted that contemporary analyses of currency problems in the interwar period were led into error by "the tacit assumption that the gold standard after the war was the same thing as the gold standard before the war."

2. This wartime experience has not been appreciated in the recent spate of articles looking at changes in the behavior of interest rates in 1914. To the extent that durable changes took place in 1914, they were much more likely to have been caused by the creation of the Federal Reserve than the "abandonment" of the gold standard. See Miron (1986), Clark (1986), and Mankiw, Miron, and Weil (1987).

3. The undoubted gain to trade would have been offset in part by the capital loss of Britain's foreign assets. De Long (1987) argued that the offset was very large.

4. This was the effect of a consolidated government budget, but the shift was almost entirely the result of federal actions.

5. The only other year the full-employment government budget was clearly expansionary was 1936, when the rest of the pension claims were paid out—over Roosevelt's veto.

6. Schuker (1988, p. 55) further denied that intervention by the United States could have rescued the German economy in 1931.

7. There also is no agreement on whether the rise in stock prices in the 1920s was a bubble. Blanchard and Wilson (1982) argued that bubbles are hard to find; Diba and Grossman (1988) claimed that rational bubbles cannot exist. White (1989) nevertheless argued that the price rises in 1928–29 constituted a bubble.

8. Bernanke (1983) argued also that there was a "progressive erosion of borrowers' collateral relative to debt burdens" that made it harder for banks to discriminate between good and bad risks, that is, that raised the cost of credit intermediation. He indexed this erosion by the magnitude of business failures, on the apparent assumption that this figure showed how close to the edge of solvency the [stable] distribution of firms was at any time.

9. These failures were not independent of the changing interest rates; they were caused in part by the lower price of bonds, which threatened the capital position of some banks and made it hard for some firms to borrow.

10. The coefficient, $a$, of $y$ in equation (7) in appendix A is positive and substantial.

11. Overy (1982) and Holtfrerich (1988) followed Borchardt's interpretation of expectations in the first phase of the Depression, while disagreeing on later developments.

12. Abraham and Katz (1986) disputed the importance of shifts in demand in the postwar period.

13. The Banks of Britain and of France may well have been afraid that the United States would devalue the dollar in 1932. They had both lost heavily in the British devaluation and were thinking of their own financial health.

14. Eichengreen and Sachs (1985) used a dummy variable for Germany and omitted the United States from most regressions. Their econometric results were due primarily to the contrast between the devaluing Scandinavian countries and the gold block. The United States would be hard to fit in their framework both because of its great size and because its devaluation was two years later than the European ones.

15. This discussion is adapted from Temin and Wigmore (1988).

16. Hardach (1980, p. 59) attributed much of the gain to the de-

layed effect of Papen and Schleicher's program, while admitting that much remains to be explained.

17. Eichengreen and Hatton (1988) used the unemployment rate of insured workers, which peaked at 44 percent. The estimate used here is the unemployment rate of industrial workers. It reflects the concept that is the most comparable to the rates calculated for the other major countries.

18. Peppers (1973) recalculated the full-employment surplus and confirmed Brown's findings.

19. Even in Russia the disastrous Soviet collectivization of agriculture signaled the dramatic end of the New Economic Policy that had given the market a relatively free rein.

20. James (1986, p. 417) dated the change to 1934–35.

21. James (1986, p. 416) said wages fell from 57 to 52 percent. Maier (1987, p. 101) said they fell from 66 to 55 percent.

22. Maier (1987, p. 98n) calculated from the same data as Overy that net private fixed investment was essentially zero through 1936. The rise in private investment was primarily inventory accumulation.

23. White (1986) argued that the combination promoted stability by allowing banks to diversify their portfolios.

24. The New Deal also created programs to employ young workers directly. The Civilian Conservation Corps was hardly the same as the Nazi compulsory labor service. It did, however, provide activity for a large segment of otherwise unemployed youth. Whether they should be considered employed in the conventional use of that term, however, is a contested question (Darby 1976; Kesselman and Savin 1978).

25. Lucas and Rapping (1969) argued that unemployment during the Depression in the United States was largely voluntary. Workers chose to consume more leisure as a result of low anticipated real interest rates. Their views have been hotly contested in the literature (Baily 1983). I have little sympathy with the view that the massive unemployment in the Depression was voluntary in any meaningful sense of the term. I therefore focus more on the actions of those workers who were employed than those who were not.

26. Bernstein (1987, p. 146) argued that structural unemployment added to the woes of American labor. This seems unlikely. The structural change was not larger than normal, and unemployment fell precipitously during World War II in the face of further structural readjustment (Gordon 1988).

27. Benjamin and Kochin (1979) argued that British workers chose to take the dole rather than work. This view has been vigorously disputed. See Benjamin and Kochin (1982) and the works cited there. More recent work has stressed the factors emphasized here: the role of demand and in particular of real wages (Broadberry 1983; Beenstock and Warburton 1986; Eichengreen 1987; Hatton 1988).

28. The problem was that AT&T used average-cost pricing as a regulated monopoly which created profit opportunities for free-standing firms offering single services. Their costs were roughly equal to AT&T's marginal cost for these services, far below its average cost. The FCC refused to allow AT&T to use marginal-cost pricing, forcing it to hold a price umbrella over the entrants (Temin and Peters 1985).

29. I do not want to equate the United States under Reagan with Germany under the Nazis; there are many other differences between the 1930s and the 1980s.

# Bibliography

Abraham, Katherine G., and Lawrence F. Katz. 1986. "Cyclical Unemployment: Sectoral Shifts or Aggregate Disturbances?" *Journal of Political Economy* 94: 507–522 (June).

Akerlof, George A., and Janet Yellen. 1986. *Efficiency Wage Models of the Labor Market*. Cambridge: Cambridge University Press.

Aldcroft, Derek H. 1970. *The Inter-war Economy: Britain, 1919–1939*. New York: Columbia University Press.

Bagehot, Walter. 1873. *Lombard Street*. New York: Scribner, Armstrong.

Baily, Martin Neil. 1983. "The Labor Market in the 1930s." *Macroeconomics, Prices, and Quantities: Essays in Memory of Arthur M. Okun*, edited by James Tobin. Washington: Brookings Institution.

Balderston, Theodore. 1977. "The German Business Cycle in the 1920's: A Comment." *Economic History Review* 30: 159–161 (February).

Balderston, Theodore. 1982. "The Origins of Economic Instability in Germany, 1924–30: Market Forces versus Economic Policy." *Vierteljahrschrift für Sozial- und Wirtschaftsgeschichte* 69: 488–512.

Balderston, Theodore. 1983. "The Beginning of the Depression in Germany, 1927–30: Investment and the Capital Market." *Economic History Review* 36: 395–414 (August).

Balderston, Theodore. 1988. "German Banking Data." Unpublished manuscript. Manchester, England.

Barber, William J. 1985. *From New Era to New Deal: Herbert Hoover, the Economists and American Economic Policy, 1921–1933.* Cambridge: Cambridge University Press.

Beenstock, Michael, and Peter Warburton. 1986. "Wages and Unemployment in Interwar Britain." *Explorations in Economic History* 23: 153–172 (April).

Benjamin, Daniel K., and Lewis A. Kochin. 1979. "Searching for an Explanation of Unemployment in Interwar Britain." *Journal of Political Economy* 87: 441–478 (June).

Benjamin, Daniel K., and Levis A. Kochin. 1982. "Unemployment and Unemployment Benefits in Twentieth Century Britain: A Reply to Our Critics." *Journal of Political Economy* 90: 410–436 (April).

Bennett, Edward W. 1962. *Germany and the Diplomacy of the Financial Crisis, 1931.* Cambridge, MA: Harvard University Press.

Bernanke, Ben. 1983. "Nonmonetary Effects of the Financial Crisis in the Propagation of the Great Depression." *American Economic Review* 73: 257–276 (June).

Bernstein, Michael A. 1987. *The Great Depression: Delayed Recovery and Economic Change in America, 1929–1939.* Cambridge: Cambridge University Press.

Blanchard, Olivier Jean. 1988. "Unemployment: Getting the Questions Right—and Some of the Answers." Paper prepared for the Chelwood Gate Conference on Unemployment, May 1988.

Blanchard, Olivier J., and Lawrence H. Summers. 1986. "Hysteresis and the European Unemployment Problem." *NBER Macroeconomics Annual 1986*, edited by Stanley Fischer. Cambridge, MA: MIT Press.

Blanchard, Olivier J., and Mark W. Watson. 1982. "Bubbles, Rational Expectations, and Financial Markets." *Crises in the Economic and Financial Structure*, edited by Paul Wachtel. Lexington, MA: D. C. Heath.

Booth, Alan. 1987. "Britain in the 1930s: A Managed Economy?" *Economic History Review* 40: 499–522 (November).

Borchardt, Knut. 1979. "Zwangslagen und Handlungspieläume in der grossen Wirtschaftskrise der fühen dreissiger

Jahre: Zur Revision des überlieferten Geschichtsbildes." *Jahrbuch der Bayerischen Akademie der Wissenschaften*. Munich.

Borchardt, Knut. 1980. "Zur Frage der Währungspolitischen Optionen Deutschlands in der Weltwirtschaftskrise." *Theorie und Politik der internationalen Wirtschaftsbeziehungen*, edited by K. Borchardt and F. Holzheu. Stuttgart: Hans Moller.

Borchardt, Knut. 1984. "Could and Should Germany Have Followed Great Britain in Leaving the Gold Standard?" *Journal of European Economic History* 13: 471–497 (Winter).

Boskin, Michael J. 1988. "Consumption, Saving, and Fiscal Policy." *American Economic Review, Proceedings* 78: 401–418 (May).

Broadberry, Steven N. 1983. "Unemployment in Interwar Britain: A Disequilibrium Approach." *Oxford Economic Papers* 35: 463–485 (November).

Broadberry, Steven N. 1984. "Fiscal Policy in Britain during the 1930s." *Economic History Review* 37: 95–102 (February).

Broadberry, Steven N. 1987. "Cheap Money and the Housing Boom in Interwar Britain: An Econometric Appraisal." *Manchester School* 55: 378–391 (December).

Brown, W. A. 1940. *The International Gold Standard Reinterpreted*. New York: National Bureau of Economic Research.

Brown, E. Cary. 1956. "Fiscal Policy in the Thirties: A Reappraisal." *American Economic Review* 46: 857–879 (December).

Bry, Gerhard. 1960. *Wages in Germany*. Princeton: Princeton University Press.

Cairncross, Alec, and Barry Eichengreen. 1983. *Sterling in Decline: The Devaluations of 1931, 1949 and 1967*. Oxford: Blackwell.

Chandler, Lester V. 1971. *American Monetary Policy, 1928–1941*. New York: Harper and Row.

Child, Frank C. 1958. *The Theory and Practice of Exchange Control in Germany*. The Hague: Martinus Nijhoff.

Childers, Thomas. 1983. *The Nazi Voter: The Social Foundations of Fascism in Germany, 1919–1933*. Chapel Hill: University of North Carolina Press.

Churchill, Winston S. 1948. *The Second World War: The Gathering Storm*. Vol. 1. Boston: Houghton Mifflin.

*Citibank Data Bank*. 1988. New York: Citibank.

Clark, Truman. 1986. "Interest Rate Seasonality and the Federal Reserve." *Journal of Political Economy* 94: 76–125 (February).

Clarke, Stephen V. O. 1967. *Central Bank Cooperation, 1924–31*. New York: Federal Reserve Bank of New York.

Commodity Research Bureau. 1939. *Commodity Yearbook, 1939*. New York: Commodity Research Bureau.

Dam W., Kenneth. 1982. *The Rules of the Game: Reform and Evolution in the International Monetary System*. Chicago: University of Chicago Press.

Darby, Michael. 1976. "Three-and-a-Half Million U.S. Employees have been Mislaid; or, An Explanation of Unemployment, 1934–41." *Journal of Political Economy* 84: 1–16 (February).

Davis, J. Ronnie. 1971. *The New Economics and the Old Economics*. Ames: Iowa State University Press.

De Long, J. Bradford. 1987. *Returning to the Gold Standard: A Macroeconomic History of Britain and France in the 1920s*. Unpublished Ph.D. dissertation. Cambridge, MA: Harvard University.

De Long, J. Bradford, and Lawrence H. Summers. 1986. "Is Increased Price Flexibility Stabilizing?" *American Economic Review* 76: 1031–1044 (December).

Diamond, Peter, and Drew Fudenberg. 1989. "Rational Expectations Business Cycles in Search Equilibrium." *Journal of Political Economy* 97: 606–619 (June).

Diba, Behzad T., and Herschel I. Grossman. 1988. "Explosive Rational Bubbles in Stock Prices?" *American Economic Review* 78: 520–530 (June).

Dixit, Avinash, and Joseph E. Stiglitz. 1977. "Monopolistic Competition and Optimum Product Diversity." *American Economic Review* 67: 297–308 (June).

Dominguez, Kathryn M., Ray C. Fair and Matthew D. Shapiro. 1988. "Forecasting the Depression: Harvard versus Yale." *American Economic Review* 78: 595–612 (September).

Dornbusch, Rudiger, and Stanley Fischer. 1986. "The Open Economy: Implications for Monetary and Fiscal Policy." *The American Business Cycle: Continuity and Change*, edited by Robert J. Gordon. Chicago: University of Chicago Press.

Eichengreen, Barry. 1986a. "The Bank of France and the Sterilization of Gold, 1926–1932." *Explorations in Economics History* 23: 56–84 (January).

Eichengreen, Barry. 1986b. "Understanding 1921–1927: Inflation and Economic Recovery in the 1920s." *Revista di Storia Economica* 3: 34–66 (International Issue).

Eichengreen, Barry. 1987. "Unemployment in Interwar Britain: Dole or Doldrums?" *Oxford Economic Papers* 39: 597–623 (December).

Eichengreen, Barry. 1989. "The Political Economy of the Smoot-Hawley Tariff." *Research in Economic History*, forthcoming.

Eichengreen, Barry, and Timothy J. Hatton. 1988. "Interwar Unemployment in International Perspective: Introduction to the Issues." *Interwar Unemployment in International Perspective*, edited by Barry Eichengreen and T. J. Hatton. Dordecht: Kluwer Academic Publishers.

Eichengreen, Barry, and Jeffrey Sachs. 1985. "Exchange Rates and Economic Recovery in the 1930s." *Journal of Economic History* 45: 925–946 (December).

Eichengreen, Barry, and Jeffrey Sachs. 1986. "Competitive Devaluation in the Great Depression: A Theoretical Reassessment." *Economic Letters* 22: 67–71 (June).

Einzig, Paul. 1932. *Behind the Scenes of International Finance*. London: Macmillan.

Ellis, Howard S. 1941. *Exchange Control in Central Europe*. Cambridge, MA: Harvard University Press.

Epstein, Gerald, and Thomas Ferguson. 1984. "Monetary Policy, Loan Liquidation and Industrial Conflict: The Federal Reserve Open Market Operation of 1932." *Journal of Economic History* 44: 957–984 (December).

Federal Reserve System. 1940. "New Federal Reserve Index of

Industrial Production." *Federal Reserve Bulletin* 26: 753–771 (August).

Federal Reserve System. 1943. *Banking and Monetary Statistics.* Washington: Government Printing Office.

Ferguson, Thomas. 1984. "From Normalcy to New Deal: Industrial Structure, Party Competition and American Public Policy in the Great Depression." *International Organizations* 38: 41–94 (Winter).

Field, Alexander J. 1984a. "Asset Exchanges and the Transactions Demand for Money, 1919–1929." *American Economic Review* 74: 43–59 (March).

Field, Alexander. 1984b. "A New Interpretation of the Onset of the Great Depression." *Journal of Economic History* 44: 489–498 (June).

Fisher, Irving. 1933. "The Debt-Deflation Theory of Great Depressions." *Econometrica* 1: 337–357.

Frankel, Jeffrey A., and Katharine Rockett. 1988. "International Macroeconomic Policy Coordination When Policymakers Do Not Agree on the True Model." *American Economic Review* 78: 318–340 (June).

Freeman, Richard B. 1988. "Contraction and Expansion: The Divergence of Private Sector and Public Sector Unionism in the United States." *Journal of Economic Perspectives* 2: 63–88 (Spring).

Fremling, Gertrud M. 1985. "Did the United Sates Transmit the Great Depression to the Rest of the World?" *American Economic Review* 75: 1181–1185 (December).

Friedman, Milton, and Anna J. Schwartz. 1963. *A Monetary History of the United States, 1867–1960.* Princeton: Princeton University Press.

Friedman, Milton, and Anna J. Schwartz. 1965. *The Great Contraction.* Princeton: Princeton University Press.

Friedman, Philip. 1974. *The Impact of Trade Destruction on National Incomes.* Gainesville, FL: The University Presses of Florida.

Galbraith, John K. 1961. *The Great Crash.* Boston: Houghton Mifflin.

Garber, Peter M. 1982. "Transition from Inflation to Price Stability." *Monetary Regimes and Protection*, Carnegie-Rochester Conference, no. 16. Amsterdam: North Holland.

Garraty, John A. 1986. *The Great Depression*. San Diego: Harcourt Brace Jovanovich.

Garvy, George. 1975. "Keynes and the Economic Activists of Pre-Hitler Germany." *Journal of Political Economy* 83: 391–405 (April).

Germany: Official Publications. 1934. *Untersuchung des Bankwesens, 1933*. 2 vols., issued by the Untersuchungausschuss für das Bankwesen. Berlin.

Germany: Official Publications. 1938. *Statistische Jahrbuch für die Deutsche Reich*. Berlin.

Gordon, Robert J. 1988. "Back to the Future: European Unemployment Today Viewed from America in 1939." *Brookings Papers on Economic Activity* 1: 271–304.

Great Britain: Parliamentary Papers. 1918. *First Interim Report of the Committee on Currency and Foreign Exchange after the War*. Cd. 9182.

Gourevitch, Peter A. 1986. *Politics in Hard Times*. Ithaca: Cornell University Press.

Grossman, Sanford J., and Oliver D. Hart. 1979. "The Costs and Benefits of Ownership: A Theory of Vertical and Lateral Integration." *Journal of Political Economy* 94: 691–719 (February).

Guillebaud, C. W. 1939. *The Economic Recovery of Germany From 1933 to the Incorporation of Austria in March 1938*. London: Macmillan.

Hall, Robert E. 1986. "The Role of Consumption in Economic Fluctuations." *The American Business Cycle: Continuity and Change*, edited by Robert J. Gordon. Chicago: University of Chicago Press.

Hamilton, James D. 1987. "Monetary Factors in the Great Depression." *Journal of Monetary Economics* 19: 145–169 (March).

Hamilton, James D. 1988. "Role of the International Gold Standard in Propagating the Great Depression." *Contemporary Policy Issues* 6: 67–89 (April).

Hamilton, Richard. 1982. *Who Voted for Hitler?* Princeton: Princeton University Press.

Hardach, Gerd. 1984. "Banking and Industry in Germany in the Interwar Period, 1919–1939." *Journal of European Economic History* 13: 201–234 (Fall).

Hardach, Karl. 1980. *The Political Economy of Germany in the Twentieth Century*. Berkeley: University of California Press.

Harrod, R. F. 1951. *The Life of John Maynard Keynes*. New York: St. Martin's Press.

Hatton, Timothy J. 1988. "A Quarterly Model of the Labour Market in Interwar Britain." *Oxford Bulletin of Economics and Statistics* 50: 1–25 (February).

Hawley, Ellis. 1966. *The New Deal and the Problem of Monopolies: A Study in Economic Ambivalence*. Princeton: Princeton University Press.

Hawtrey, Ralph G. 1938. *A Century of Bank Rate*. London: Longmans, Green.

Hayes, Peter. 1987. *Industry and Ideology: IG Farben in the Nazi Era*. Cambridge: Cambridge University Press.

Henning, Friedrich-Wilhelm. 1973. "Die zeitliche Einordnung der Überwingund der Weltwirtschaftshkrise in Deutschland." *Schriften des Vereins für Sozialpolitik* NF 135–173.

Himmelberg, Robert F. 1976. *The Origins of the National Recovery Administration*. New York: Fordham University Press.

Holtfrerich, Carl-Ludwig. 1986. *The German Inflation, 1914–1923: Causes and Effects in International Perspective*, translated by Theodore Balderston. Berlin: Walter de Gruyter.

Holtfrerich, Carl-Ludwig. 1988. "Was the Policy of Deflation in Germany Unavoidable?" Unpublished manuscript. Berlin.

Hoover, Herbert. 1952. *The Memoirs of Herbert Hoover: The Great Depression, 1929–1941*. New York: Macmillan.

Hoover, Herbert H. 1933. "Lincoln Day Address, February 13, 1933." *Commercial and Financial Chronicle* 136: 1136–1138 (February 18).

Howson, Susan. 1975. *Domestic Monetary Management in Britain, 1919–1938*. Cambridge: Cambridge University Press.

Howson, Susan. 1980. *Sterling's Managed Float: The Operations of the Exchange Equalisation Account, 1932–39*. Princeton Studies in International Finance, no. 46. Princeton: Department of Economics, Princeton University.

Howson, Susan, and Donald Winch. 1977. *The Economic Advisory Council, 1930–1939*. Cambridge: Cambridge University Press.

Jackson, Julian. 1985. *The Politics of Depression in France, 1932–1936*. Cambridge: Cambridge University Press.

James, Harold. 1984. "The Causes of the German Banking Crisis of 1931." *Economic History Review* 38: 68–87 (February).

James, Harold. 1985. *The Reichsbank and Public Finance in Germany, 1924–1933: A Study of the Politics of Economics during the Great Depression*. Frankfurt: Fritz Knapp Verlag.

James, Harold. 1986. *The German Slump: Politics and Economics, 1924–1936*. Oxford: Oxford University Press.

Jenkins, Peter. 1988. *Mrs. Thatcher's Revolution: The Ending of the Socialist Era*. Cambridge, MA: Harvard University Press.

Jensen, Richard J. 1989. "The Causes and Cures of Unemployment in the Great Depression." *Journal of Interdisciplinary History* 19: 553–584 (Spring).

Kennedy, Paul M. 1987. *The Rise and Fall of the Great Powers: Economic Change and Military Conflict from 1500 to 2000*. New York: Random House.

Kesselman, J. R., and N. E. Savin. 1978. "Three-and-a-Half Million Workers Never Were Lost." *Economic Inquiry* 16: 205–225 (April).

Keynes, John Maynard. 1922. "The Stabilization of the European Exchanges: A Plan for Genoa." *Manchester Guardian Commercial* (April 20).

Keynes, John Maynard. 1931. "An Economic Analysis of Unemployment (Harris Lectures)." Reprinted in *The Collected Writings of John Maynard Keynes*. Vol. 13, 1973, edited by Donald Moggridge. London: Macmillan.

Keynes, John Maynard. 1933. August letter to N. V. Phillips Lamp. Cambridge: Kings College Archives, Keynes Papers, BMJ/ 53.

Keyssar, Alexander. 1986. *Out of Work*. Cambridge: Cambridge University Press.

Kindleberger, Charles P. 1986. *The World In Depression, 1929– 1939*. 2d ed. Berkeley: University of California Press.

Kunz, Diane B. 1987. *The Battle for Britain's Gold Standard, 1931*. London: Croom Helm.

Lange, Oscar, and Fred M. Taylor. 1938. *On the Economic Theory of Socialism*. Reprinted, New York: McGraw-Hill, 1964.

League of Nations. 1934. *World Economic Survey, 1933–34*. Geneva: League of Nations.

Lee, Bradford A. 1982. "The New Deal Reconsidered." *Wilson Quarterly* 6 (2): 62–76 (Spring).

Lewis, W. Arthur. 1949. *Economic Survey, 1919–1939*. London: Allen and Unwin.

Lieberman, Sima. 1977. *The Growth of European Mixed Economies, 1945–1970*. New York: Wiley.

Lilien, David M. 1982. "Sectoral Shifts and Cyclical Unemployment." *Journal of Political Economy* 90: 777–793 (August).

Lindert, Peter H. 1969. *Key Currencies and Gold, 1900–1913*. Princeton Studies in International Finance, no. 24. Princeton: Department of Economics, Princeton University.

Loveman, Gary W., and Chris Tilly. 1988. "Good Jobs or Bad Jobs: What Does the Evidence Say?" *New England Economic Review*, pp. 46–65 (January/February).

Lubove, Roy. 1986. *The Struggle for Social Security, 1900–1935*. Pittsburgh: University of Pittsburgh Press.

Lucas, Robert E., Jr. 1981. *Studies in Business-Cycle Theory*. Cambridge, MA: MIT Press.

Lucas, Robert E., and Leonard A. Rapping. 1969. "Real Wages, Employment, and Inflation." *Journal of Political Economy* 77: 721– 754 (September–October).

Maier, Charles S. 1975. *Recasting Bourgeois Europe: Stabilization in France, Germany, and Italy in the Decade after World War I.* Princeton: Princeton University Press.

Maier, Charles S. 1987. *In Search of Stability.* New York: Cambridge University Press.

Mankiw, N. Gregory, Jeffrey A. Miron, and David N. Weil. 1987. "The Adjustment of Expectations to a Change in Regime: A Study of the Founding of the Federal Reserve." *American Economic Review* 77: 358–374 (June).

Matthews, K. G. P. 1986. "Was Sterling Overvalued in 1925?" *Economic History Review* 39: 572–587 (November).

Mayer, Thomas. 1980. "Consumption in the Great Depression." *Journal of Political Economy* 86: 139–145 (February).

McKibban, Ross. 1975. "The Economic Policies of the Second Labour Government, 1929–31." *Past and Present*, no. 68: 95–123 (August).

McNeil, William C. 1986. *American Money and the Weimar Republic: Economics and Politics on the Eve of the Great Depression.* New York: Columbia University Press.

Meltzer, Allen H. 1976. "Monetary and Other Explanations of the Start of the Great Depression." *Journal of Monetary Economics* 2: 455–471.

Middleton, Roger. 1981. "The Constant Employment Budget Balance and British Budgetary Policy, 1929–39." *Economic History Review* 34: 266–286 (May).

Middleton, Roger. 1984. "The Measurement of Fiscal Influence in Britain in the 1930s." *Economic History Review* 37: 103–106 (February).

Milward, Alan. 1977. *War, Economy, and Society, 1939–1945.* Berkeley: University of California Press.

Milward, Alan. 1983. "Review of Overy, *The Nazi Economic Recovery.*" *Economic History Review* 36: 652–654 (November).

Minsky, Hyman P. 1982. "The Financial-Instability Hypothesis: Capitalist Processes and the Behavior of the Economy." *Financial Crises: Theory, History, and Policy,* edited by Charles P. Kindleberger and Jean-Pierre Laffargue. Cambridge: Cambridge University Press.

Miron, Jeffrey. 1986. "Financial Panics, the Seasonality of the Nominal Interest Rate, and the Founding of the Fed." *American Economic Review* 76: 125–140 (March).

Mishkin, Frederic S. 1978. "The Household Balance Sheet and the Great Depression." *Journal of Economic History* 38: 918–937 (December).

Mitchell, B. K. 1980. *European Historical Statistics, 1750–1975*. New York: Facts on File.

Moggridge, Donald E. 1969. *The Return to Gold, 1925: The Formulation of Economic Policy and Its Critics*. Cambridge: Cambridge University Press.

Moggridge, Donald E. 1972. *British Monetary Policy, 1924–31: The Norman Conquest of $4.86*. Cambridge: Cambridge University Press.

Mowat, Charles Loch. 1955. *Britain between the Wars, 1918–1940*. Chicago: University of Chicago Press.

Muth, John F. 1961. "Rational Expectations and the Theory of Price Movements." *Econometrica* 29: 315–335 (July).

National Industrial Conference Board. 1934. *The New Monetary System of the United States*. New York: National Industrial Conference Board.

Northrop, Mildred B. 1938. *Control Policies of the Reichsbank, 1924–1933*. New York: Columbia University Press.

Nove, Alec, and D. M. Nuti. 1972. *Socialist Economics: Selected Readings*. Harmondsworth: Penguin Books.

Nurkse, Ragnar. 1944. *International Currency Experience: Lessons of the Interwar Period*. Geneva: League of Nations.

Nutter, G. Warren, and Henry Adler Einhorn. 1969. *Enterprise Monopoly in the United States: 1899–1958*. New York: Columbia University Press.

Overy, R. J. 1975. "Cars, Roads, and Economic Recovery in Germany, 1932–8." *Economic History Review* 28: 466–483 (August).

Overy, R. J. 1979. "The German Motorisierung and Rearmament: A Reply." *Economic History Review* 32: 107–112 (February).

Overy, R. J. 1982. *The Nazi Economic Recovery, 1932–1938.* London: Macmillan.

Patat, Jean-Pierre, and Michel Lutfalla. 1987. *Histoire monetaire de la France au XXe siecle.* Paris: Economica.

Peppers, L. A. 1973. "Full Employment Surplus and Structural Change: The 1930s." *Explorations in Economic History* 10: 197–210 (Winter).

Robbins, Lionel. 1934. *The Great Depression.* London: Macmillan.

Robbins, Lord (Lionel). 1971. *Autobiography of an Economist.* London: Macmillan.

Romer, Christina D. 1986. "Spurious Volatility in Historical Unemployment Data." *Journal of Political Economy* 94: 1–37 (February).

Romer, Christina D. 1988. "The Great Crash and the Onset of the Great Depression." Unpublished manuscript. Berkeley.

Rucker, Randal R., and Lee J. Alston. 1987. "Farm Failures and Government Intervention: A Case Study of the 1930's." *American Economic Review* 77: 724–730 (September).

Sargent, Thomas J. 1983. "The Ends of Four Big Inflations." *Inflation: Causes and Effects*, edited by Robert E. Hall. Chicago: University of Chicago Press.

Sargent, Thomas J. 1986. "Stopping Moderate Inflations: The Methods of Poincare and Thatcher." *Rational Expectations and Inflation*, edited by Thomas J. Sargent. New York: Harper and Row.

Sargent, Thomas, and Neil Wallace. 1975. "'Rational' Expectations, the Optimal Monetary Instrument and the Optimal Money Supply Rule." *Journal of Political Economy* 83: 241–254 (April).

Sauvy, Alfred. 1965–75. *Histoire économique de la France entre les deux guerres.* 4 vols. Paris: Fayard.

Sayers, Richard S. 1976. *The Bank of England, 1891–1944.* Cambridge: Cambridge University Press.

Schuker, Stephen A. 1976. *The End of French Predominance in*

*Europe: The Financial Crisis of 1924 and the Adoption of the Dawes Plan*. Chapel Hill: University of North Carolina Press.

Schuker, Stephen A. 1988. *American "Reparations" to Germany, 1919–33: Implications for the Third-World Debt Crisis*, Princeton Studies in International Finance, no. 61. Princeton: Department of Economics, Princeton University.

Schwartz, Anna J. 1981. "Understanding 1929–33." *The Great Depression Revisited*, edited by Karl Brunner. The Hague: Martinus Nijhoff.

Shiller, Robert J. 1981. "Do Stock Prices Move Too Much to Be Justified by Subsequent Changes in Dividends?" *American Economic Review* 71: 421–436 (June).

Silverman, Dan P. 1982. *Reconstructing Europe after the Great War*. Cambridge, MA: Harvard University Press.

Solow, Robert M. 1985. "Economic History and Economics." *American Economic Review, Proceedings* 75: 328–331 (May).

Spence, A. Michael. 1974. *Market Signaling*. Cambridge, MA: Harvard University Press.

Spenceley, G. F. F. 1979. "R. J. Overy and the Motorisierung: A Comment." *Economic History Review* 32: 100–106 (February).

Sprague, O. M. W. 1910. *History of Crises under the National Banking System*. Washington: Government Printing Office.

Stachura, Peter. 1986. "Introduction." *Unemployment and the Great Depression in Germany*, edited by Peter Stachura. London: Macmillan.

Stein, Herbert. 1969. *The Fiscal Revolution in America*. Chicago: University of Chicago Press.

Stiefel, Dieter. 1989. *Finanzdiplomatie und Weltwirtschaftskrise: Die Krise der Credit-Anstalt 1931 und ihre wirtschaftlich-politische Bewaltigung*. Frankfort: Knapp Verlag.

Stiglitz, Joseph E., and Andrew Weiss. 1981. "Credit Rationing in Markets with Imperfect Information." *American Economic Review* 71: 393–410 (June).

Stolper, Gustav, Karl Häuser, and Knut Borchardt. 1967. *The*

*German Economy, 1870 to the Present.* New York: Harcourt Brace and World.

Studenski, Paul, and Herman E. Krooss. 1963. *Financial History of the United States.* 2d ed. New York: McGraw-Hill.

Svennilson, Ingvar. 1954. *Growth and Stagnation in the European Economy.* Geneva: United Nations Economic Commission for Europe.

Swanson, Joseph, and Samuel Williamson. 1972. "Estimates of National Product and Income for the United States, 1919–1941." *Explorations in Economic History* 10: 53–73 (Fall).

Taft, Philip. 1964. *Organized Labor in American History.* New York: Harper and Row.

Taylor, John. 1979. "Staggered Wage Setting in a Macro Model." *American Economic Review, Proceedings* 69: 108–113 (May).

Temin, Peter. 1971. "The Beginning of the Depression in Germany." *Economic History Review* 24: 240–248 (May).

Temin, Peter. 1976. *Did Monetary Forces Cause the Great Depression?* New York: Norton.

Temin, Peter. 1980. *Taking Your Medicine: Drug Regulation in the United States.* Cambridge, MA: Harvard University Press.

Temin, Peter. 1981. "Notes on the Causes of the Great Depression." *The Great Depression Revisited,* edited by Karl Brunner. The Hague: Martinus Nijhoff.

Temin, Peter. 1982. "The Impact of the Depression on Economic Thought." *Economics in the Long View: Models and Methodology,* edited by Charles P. Kindleberger and Guido di Tella. Vol. 1. London: Macmillan.

Temin, Peter. 1987. *The Fall of the Bell System.* Cambridge: Cambridge University Press.

Temin, Peter. 1988. "Free Land and Federalism: American Economic Exceptionalism." Department of Economics Working Paper 481. Cambridge, MA: MIT (February).

Temin, Peter, and Geoffrey Peters. 1985. "Cross-Subsidization in the Telephone Network." *Willamette Law Review* 21: 199–223 (Spring).

Temin, Peter, and Barrie Wigmore. 1988. "The End of One Big Deflation, 1933." Department of Economics Working Paper 503. Cambridge, MA: MIT (October).

Thorp, W. L., and W. F. Crowder. 1941. *The Structure of Industry*. Monograph no. 27. Temporary National Economic Committee. Washington: Government Printing Office.

Tobin, James. 1975. "Keynesian Models of Recession and Depression." *American Economic Review, Proceedings* 65: 195–202 (May).

U.S. Bureau of the Census. 1975. *Historical Statistics of the United States, Colonial Times to 1970*. Washington: Government Printing Office.

van der Wee, Herman. 1986. *Prosperity and Upheaval: The World Economy, 1945–1980*. New York: Viking.

Vickers, John, and George Yarrow. 1988. *Privatization: An Economic Analysis*. Cambridge, MA: MIT Press.

Wardell, William M. (ed.). 1978. *Controlling the Uses of Therapeutic Drugs: An International Comparison*. Washington: American Enterprise Institute.

Warsh, David. 1988. "The Man in the Silver Tower." *Boston Globe Magazine* pp. 16–17, 69–91 (September 11).

Weinstein, Michael M. 1980. *Recovery and Redistribution under the NIRA*. Amsterdam: North Holland.

Wheelock, David C. 1988. "The Demand for Federal Reserve Credit: The Key to Fed Errors in the Great Depression?" Department of Economics Working Paper 88–3. Austin: University of Texas.

White, Eugene N. 1984. "A Reinterpretation of the Banking Crisis of 1930." *Journal of Economic History* 44: 119–138 (March).

White, Eugene N. 1986. "Before the Glass-Steagall Act: An Analysis of the Investment Banking Activities of National Banks." *Explorations in Economic History* 23: 33–55 (January).

White, Eugene N. 1989. "When the Ticker Ran Late: The Stock Market Boom and Crash of 1929." *The Stock Market Crash in Historical Perspective*, edited by Eugene N. White. Homewood, IL: Dow-Jones Irwin.

Wicker, Elmus R. 1966. *Federal Reserve Monetary Policy, 1917–1933*. New York: Random House.

Wicker, Elmus R. 1980. "A Reconsideration of the Causes of the Banking Panic of 1930." *Journal of Economic History* 40: 571–583 (September).

Wicker, Elmus. 1982. "Interest Rate and Expenditure Effects of the Banking Crisis of 1930." *Explorations in Economic History* 19: 435–445 (October).

Wicker, Elmus. 1986. "Terminating Hyperinflation in the Dismembered Habsburg Monarchy." *American Economic Review* 76: 350–364 (June).

Wigmore, Barrie A. 1985. *The Crash and Its Aftermath: A History of Securities Markets in the United States, 1929–1933*. Westport, CT: Greenwood Press.

Wigmore, Barrie A. 1987. "Was the Bank Holiday of 1933 Caused by a Run on the Dollar?" *Journal of Economic History* 47: 739–755 (September).

Winch, Donald. 1969. *Economics and Policy: A Historical Study*. New York: Walker.

Witte, Eberhard. 1988. *Restructuring of the [German] Telecommunications System*. Report of the Government Commission for Telecommunications. Heidelberg: R. v. Decker's Verlag.

Worswick, G. D. N. 1984. "The Sources of Economic Recovery in the U.K. in the 1930s." *National Institute Economic Review* no. 110: 85–93 (November).

Youngson, A. J. 1960. *The British Economy, 1920–1957*. Cambridge, MA: Harvard University Press.

# Index